S T . I G N A T I U S L O Y O L A

Ladislaus Lukacs, S.J., "Ratio atque institutio studiorum Societatis Iesu," general
introduction to *Monumenta Paedagogica Societatis Iesu*, vol. 5 (Rome: Institutum
Historicum Societatis Iesu, 1986), pp. 1-36.
Translated, edited, and published with permission of Institutum Historicum Societatis Iesu.

Giuseppe Cosentino, "Le matematiche nella *Ratio Studiorum* della Compagnia di Gesù,"
Miscellanea Storica Ligure, 2, new series, no. 2 (1970), pp. 171-213.
Translated, edited and published with permission of Università di Genova, Instituto di
Storia Moderna e Contemporanea.

Giuseppe Cosentino, "L'Insegnamento delle matematiche nei collegi gesuitici nell'Italia
settentrionale: Nota introduttiva," *Physis*, 13 (1971), pp. 205-17.
Translated, edited, and published with permission of Casa Editrice Leo S. Olschki.

ISBN 0-916101-30-4 paper

Published by:

SAINT JOSEPH'S UNIVERSITY PRESS
5600 City Avenue
Philadelphia, Pennsylvania 19131-1395
www.sju.edu/sjupress/

Saint Joseph's University Press is a member of the Association of Jesuit University Presses

Library of Congress Cataloging-in-Publication Data

Church, culture, and curriculum: theology and mathematics in the
Ratio studiorum / translated by Frederick A. Homann.
    p. cm.
    Includes bibliographical references (p.   ).
    Contents: A history of the Jesuit Ratio studiorum / Ladislaus
Lukács—Mathematics in the Jesuit Ratio studiorum / Giuseppe
Cosentino—Mathematics instruction in Jesuit colleges of northern
Italy.
    ISBN 0-916101-30-4
    1. Jesuits. Ratio studiorum. 2. Theology—Study and teaching—
History. 3. Mathematics—Study and teaching (Higher)—History.
I. Homann, Frederick A. II. Lukács, Ladislaus. Ratio atque
institutio studiorum Societatis Iesu. English. III. Cosentino,
Giuseppe, 1950- Matematiche nella "Ratio studiorum" della
Compagnia di Gesù. English. IV. Cosentino, Giuseppe, 1950-
Mathematics instruction in Jesuit colleges of northern Italy.
English.
BX3704.Z5C55 1999
230' .07'32—dc21
                                              99-29173
                                                CIP

Cover illustration: Stained glass medallion, St. Barbara's Church, Philadelphia.

Frontispiece: *St. Ignatius Loyola*, 19th c., copper engraving, The Peters Collection,
Saint Joseph's University.

CHURCH, CULTURE & CURRICULUM

THEOLOGY AND MATHEMATICS
IN THE JESUIT *RATIO STUDIORUM*

LADISLAUS LUKACS, S.J.

AND

GIUSEPPE COSENTINO

TRANSLATED AND EDITED WITH AN INTRODUCTION BY

FREDERICK A. HOMANN, S.J.

SAINT JOSEPH'S UNIVERSITY PRESS, PHILADELPHIA
MEMBER OF THE ASSOCIATION OF JESUIT UNIVERSITY PRESSES

Table of Contents

Introduction
Frederick A. Homann, S.J.

1

A History of the Jesuit *Ratio Studiorum*
Ladislaus Lukacs, S.J.

17

Mathematics in the Jesuit *Ratio Studiorum*
Giuseppe Cosentino

47

Mathematics Instruction in Jesuit Colleges of Northern Italy
Giuseppe Cosentino

81

INTRODUCTION

Frederick A. Homann, S.J.

THE *RATIO STUDIORUM* 1599-1999

Three seminal essays on early Jesuit education and academic freedom in theology and mathematics, by Father Ladislaus Lukacs, S.J., and Professor Giuseppe Cosentino, are offered here in English translation to help mark the four-hundredth anniversary of the *Ratio studiorum*. That renown study plan of the Society of Jesus, promulgated in 1599, regulated Jesuit academies from grammar school up to seminary and university level worldwide until well into the twentieth century. Several recent conferences here and abroad used the 1999 anniversary not only to review the history and pervasive influence of the *Ratio studiorum* from 1599 to now, but most of all to survey the present state of Jesuit founded programs, in particular on the undergraduate university level, and to estimate their prospects and value in the Society's apostolic mission in the new millennium. The Lukacs and Cosentino essays can foster such efforts, by providing useful data and critical perspective on the recurring tasks and contemporary challenges for Jesuit teachers and their many colleagues, besides helping to fill out the larger picture of post-Renaissance European pedagogy and science.

June 1999 saw the international conference "Jesuit Education 21: The Future of Jesuit Higher Education" convoked at Saint Joseph's University in Philadelphia. The convention, which took the opportunity to mark the *Ratio studiorum* anniversary, followed up publication of *Promise Renewed: Jesuit Higher Education for a New Millennium* (Chicago: Loyola Press, 1999). Edited by Martin R. Tripole, S.J., *Promise Renewed* comprises an impressive collection of essays written by American Jesuit university scholars from a wide spectrum of disciplines. Each explained how he answered the invitation of the Society's 34th General Congregation in 1995 to locate and energize his own professional work relative to both the

1

overall Jesuit mission today and to shared apostolic efforts in university teaching and scholarly research that are rooted in the *Ratio studiorum*.

Their intellectual apostolate today continues what the Society's founder and first Superior General, St. Ignatius Loyola, sanctioned in the *General Constitutions* that he composed for the Society from 1540 to 1556. After the death of St. Ignatius, and mindful of his promise of fuller attention to this crucial matter, the Society's first five General Congregations regulated the rapidly expanding Jesuit educational apostolate with a series of provisional directives. Those initiatives eventuated in 1599 in the *Ratio atque Institutio Studiorum Societatis Iesu (The Plan and Implementation of Academic Faculties of the Society of Jesus)*. The document, promulgated from Rome by the fifth Superior General, Father Claude Acquaviva, and sometimes called Acquaviva's *Ratio studiorum*, applied to the whole Society. Because it had its promise and origin in the *General Constitutions*, the *Ratio* was treasured among the Fundamentals of the Institute of the Society. Its influence and effects in and out of Jesuit schools were immediate and immense.

Both Lukacs and Cosentino consider, though in supplementary ways and with different goals in mind, the developmental history of the 1599 *Ratio*. Importantly, each one highlights a distinct special strand against the overall history. As their essays show, its publication came after numerous draft versions, innumerable committee meetings, occasional directives of a Superior General, wide consultation of the Jesuit schools and provinces, interventions by special interest groups and external events, close consideration by early Jesuit General Congregations, and almost frenetic activity in the experience and practice of countless Jesuits, as teachers, administrators, and students. Truly a prophetic paradigm for the experience of the turn-of-the-millennium Jesuit educational plans and practice described in *Promise Renewed*.

A HISTORY OF THE *RATIO STUDIORUM*

The lead paper, Father Ladislaus Lukacs' "A History of the Jesuit *Ratio studiorum*," is an abridged English translation of his *Introductio generalis (pp. 1*-36*)* to *Monumenta Paedagogica Societatis Iesu, tom.* V (Rome: Institutum Historicum Societatis Iesu, 1986.). Lukacs, a member of the Institutum Historicum Societatis Iesu (Institute of Jesuit History) in Rome and prior to his death in 1998, the foremost expert on the history of the *Ratio*, edited the volume to mark the 400th anniversary of publication of the provisional 1586 text *Ratio atque institutio studiorum*.

Its 500 pages provide the principal documents in the various Roman archives of the Society associated with the 1586, 1591, and 1599 draft versions of the *Ratio studiorum*. Along with the six companion volumes (I-IV, VI-VII) in the *Monumenta Paedagogica* series that Lukacs also edited, it is an indispensable resource for *Ratio* history.

Lukacs' *Introductio generalis* is neither well known nor readily accessible to Latin-challenged American Jesuit educational circles. It was primarily intended to be a new account of the overall development of the *Ratio studiorum* as a cooperative Jesuit project. There are still no comparably documented studies of that effort either in English or any other language. But his paper also, necessarily and happily, describes a particular development strand that has to be considered the most crucial one in *Ratio* history, that is, the intense, prolonged struggle in the early Society over the specific content of the curriculum in speculative theology and the appropriate academic freedom in treating disputed doctrinal questions and in espousing probable theological opinions that ought to be accorded its professors in their writing and public lectures.

The struggle, naturally, was not an entirely internal affair. The Roman Jesuits, as Lukacs' history relates, could not but be influenced in their decisions by the Spanish Inquisition's seizure of draft copies of the 1586 *Ratio*. Along with lists of prescribed and optional theses in theology, the copies had been sent to the provinces for their comments and approval. (All were later returned to the Society, thanks to the intervention of Pope Sixtus V.) Mindful too of St. Ignatius' experience with the Spanish Inquisition at Alcalá and Salamanca, when he was imprisoned and questioned about his doctrine in the *Spiritual Exercises,* the Society consulted the Holy See about the proposal to publish in connection with the *Ratio* a manual of Thomistic theses. Excerpted from Aquinas' *Summa Theologica,* the compendium was to govern Jesuit teaching of theological doctrine. (Interestingly, the Roman Inquisition's reviewer judged the proposal to print the manual inappropriate insofar as that might have a chilling effect on the freedom of other theologians to hold opinions that differed from those of St. Thomas.) The Society handled the question of academic freedom pragmatically, and somewhat uneasily, as we learn from Lukacs, and the controversy lay dormant behind the *Ratio* chapters that were to regulate the teaching of theology as the crowning part of a Jesuit university program intended to be a prime instance of evangelization and of service to the Church.

Lukacs' *Introductio generalis* does not relate comparable debates about the presence and function in the curriculum of languages (Greek, Hebrew,

Syriac, etc.), or of the classical-medieval trivium (grammar, rhetoric, logic) and quadrivium (arithmetic, geometry, music, astronomy), or of philosophy. Fortunately, to supplement the story of the theological disciplines, Cosentino accounts for the mathematical sciences of the quadrivium. Analogous accounts for grammar, rhetoric, logic, natural philosophy, and metaphysics can be developed by consulting the documents and references in the *Monumenta Paedagogica* volumes. Each of those now almost forgotten debates aimed at refining Jesuit and extern academic experience into a program to form both contemporary Jesuit and extern students in keeping with the Ignatian vision and the Society's primary apostolic mission of service to the Church and the defense of the Catholic faith, as both Lukacs and Cosentino observe.

Publication of the *Ratio* did not, of course, end the controversy or resolve the underlying problems of academic freedom in the university. The Roman Inquisition's controversial proscription of Copernicus and the condemnation of Galileo in the early seventeenth century again raised issues about interpretation of Scripture and Church doctrine and how much freedom Jesuit theologians, natural philosophers, and mathematicians had to treat such matters in the public forum. Similar controversies involving the faith and unsettled doctrinal positions soon followed. Most notable prior to the Suppression of the Society in 1773 were the controversies with Dominican theologians and the Calvinists about predestination and divine foreknowledge, as well as the struggle with Pascal and the Jansenists about the licitness of following probable opinions in moral theology and cases of conscience.

Today, the question of academic freedom for the Society, and for Catholic theologians generally, involves the need to determine what theological doctrines are legitimately open to debate, and at what point dissent from Church teaching becomes unacceptable. In the aftermath of Vatican Council II and Pope Paul VI's 1968 encyclical *Humanae Vitae,* the Society's 34th General Congregation addressed the issue, in an attempt to provide guidance for theology professors, and Jesuits generally, in a very neuralgic ecclesiastical milieu. Faith-freedom tensions have been with the Society in all its apostolic work from its very inception, as may be surmised from the explicit "Rules for thinking with the Church" that St. Ignatius attached to his *Spiritual Exercises,* the foundational document for the Society and its *General Constitutions.* St. Ignatius had not forgotten Alcalá, Salamanca, and the Spanish Inquisition.

MATHEMATICS IN THE *RATIO STUDIORUM*

Professor Giuseppe Cosentino's study, "Le matematiche nelle *Ratio studiorum* della Compagnia di Gesù" ("Mathematics in the Jesuit *Ratio studiorum*"), *Miscellanea Storica Ligure*, 2, new series, no. 2 (1970), pp. 171-213 (English translation: this volume, pp. 47-79), examines another notably important but today virtually unknown strand in *Ratio* history. This was the dispute over the role and importance in the Jesuit educational program that the *Ratio* was to accord the classical quadrivium disciplines of arithmetic, geometry, music (applied arithmetic), and astronomy (applied geometry), and their derivative sciences such as optics, perspective, and ecclesiastical calendar computation *(computus ecclesiasticus).*

An especially sensitive issue was the place these disciplines were to have in the arts, or philosophy, faculty in the Society's Roman College. (Founded in 1551 by St. Ignatius primarily for Jesuit students, the Collegio Romano was granted university status in 1581 and generously endowed by Pope Gregory XIII. Over its door was the inscription "School of Grammar, Humanities, and Christian Doctrine, gratis." Its early history is closely linked with that of the *Ratio;* it operates today as the Pontifical Gregorian University.) In the mind of St. Ignatius, the Collegio Romano was to be the mother and model for all Jesuit colleges and universities, and its practice would shape that of daughter schools throughout the world. But the prestige first accorded the Roman College, and St. Ignatius' choice in the *General Constitutions* of Aristotle's system for Jesuit philosophical doctrine, gave its faculty of philosophy a platform to mount a challenge to the presence of mathematics in the curriculum there and elsewhere.

With a predominantly conservative Aristotelian orientation, and at best reluctant to assign intrinsic scientific value (in the Aristotelian sense of science [*scientia*] as knowledge through causes) to mathematical reasoning, the Roman College philosophers were all too often ignorant and entirely contemptuous of the discipline, as their preeminent mathematician colleague Christopher Clavius sadly observed. Heated debate quickly ensued among the College faculty about the prominent role for the mathematical sciences in the Society's university program championed by Baldassarre Torres (the College's first mathematics professor), Jerome Nadal, who as rector at Messina had developed its mathematics curriculum, and the scientifically prolific Clavius.

Like the internal Roman College dialog about academic freedom and the theology syllabus, the debate about the role of mathematics was also significantly shaped by external circumstances, in this case a sixteenth-century dispute between humanists, mathematicians, and philosophers that Professor Neal W. Gilbert first drew modern attention to in his *Renaissance Concepts of Method* (New York: Columbia University Press, 1961). The University of Padua Averroists (radical Aristotelians) precipitated an epistemological controversy about the nature of proof *(demonstratio)* and the validity of the conclusions in mathematics, especially in geometry. The controversy intensified in 1547 with the publication of Alessandro Piccolomini's *Commentarium de certitudine mathematicarum disciplinarum (Essay on Certitude in Mathematics)* to engage a broad spectrum of mathematicians and philosophers. Persisting in Italian academic circles, Jesuit ones included, long after promulgation of the 1599 *Ratio,* the bitter struggle came to involve, besides Clavius and his Roman College Aristotelian antagonists, colleague Benedict Pereira in particular, several prominent seventeenth-century Jesuit mathematicians. The most notable was Josephus Blancanus (Giuseppe Biancani), who had been a student in the Mathematics Academy Clavius established at the Roman College. Later as professor at Bologna, he advanced Clavius' efforts to establish Euclidean geometry as a true Aristotelian science in his 1615 metamathematical treatise, *De mathematicarum natura dissertatio (Essay on the Nature of Mathematics)*.

The *De certitudine* dispute figures appropriately in the 1970 paper that Cosentino, a member of the Domus Galilaeana Institute in Pisa, published on the *Ratio* as part of the Institute's history of science and mathematics research program, and whose studies center on sixteenth and seventeenth-century Italian institutions and practitioners, the University of Padua, Galileo and the Jesuits, Bellarmine, Biancani, Pereira, the Collegio Romano, and the Roman Inquisition.

Drawing on Jesuit archives as well as constitutions, syllabi, and pedagogical practice of established French, Spanish, and Italian universities, along with standard contemporary commentaries and texts, Cosentino fashioned a matrix for evaluation of the significance that Jesuit mathematical practice, derived from implementation of the *Ratio,* had for the history of early modern European science and mathematics education. At the same time he set the context for the measure of Jesuit scientists in the new European intellectual life and scientific methodology of the seventeenth century, the age of Galileo and the Scientific Revolution. His work has been taken up by several American historians who have looked at Jesuit science and mathematics of the time, notably by Father William A. Wallace, O.P., and Professors Edward Grant, John Heilbron, Steve Harris, James Lattis, et al.

Many distinguished Jesuit names in the debates about the teaching of theology and the role of mathematics in the philosophy program comprise a common element in Lukacs and Cosentino. St. Ignatius, Juan de Polanco and Diego Ledesma, Francis Borgia and Claude Acquaviva, Francisco Suárez and Robert Bellarmine, Jerome Nadal and Christopher Clavius, all are key figures in the two accounts. Admitted to the Society in 1555 by St. Ignatius himself, Clavius is remembered today especially for his work on the Gregorian Calendar reform of 1582 that exemplified the Church's role in fashioning social structure and reality. Bellarmine the theologian, now canonized and a Doctor of the Church, later consulted Clavius the mathematician about Galileo's use of the telescope to support Copernicus' heliocentrism, as geometric astronomy prepared to challenge the Church's reading of the Scriptures and Aristotelian epistemology. Each *Ratio* participant contributed in substantial measure to the Society's early intellectual apostolate, to provide a rich legacy for their successors, early and late, Jesuit and lay, mathematician, philosopher, or theologian, in their crucial work of service to the Church and inculturation of the faith. Each helped put intellect in the service of Christ the King, in a Europe divided by the Reformation and anticipating the Enlightenment, in a China that welcomed Matteo Ricci bearing Clavius' geometry and astronomy, no less than in the missions of the New World that needed to learn how to compute the date of Easter each year.

THE *MODUS PARISIENSIS*

Jesuit academic work began at Messina, Sicily, as a spiritual work of service to the neighbor and an inculturation of the Catholic faith in a late Mediterranean Renaissance milieu. It soon reached Spain, Italy, Germany and the North. Cosentino, then, like Lukacs, has to consider the internal history of *Ratio* pedagogy both in terms of the apostolic norms of the *General Constitutions* and of the pedagogical resources which the times and places offered that work. The *modus parisiensis,* the "Parisian style" of educational administration with a humanist bias, became an especially important resource for the Society.

Parisian methods impressed St. Ignatius and his first Jesuit companions, and Jerome Nadal too. All were Masters of Arts of the University of Paris, and well disposed to have Jesuit schools adapt freely the University's humanist and pedagogical traditions to their own apostolic goals. Father George Ganss, S.J., described their mindset in his monograph *St. Ignatius' Idea of a Jesuit University* (Milwaukee: Marquette University Press, 1954).

Later, though less accessibly to English-only readers, Father Gabriel Codina-Mir, an Institutum Historicum Societatis Iesu colleague of Father Lukacs, provided *Ratio* scholars, Cosentino and Lukacs included, an invaluable resource in his monograph *Aux sources de la pedagogie des Jésuites: Le "Modus parisiensis"* (Rome: Institutum Historicum Societatis Iesu, 1968).

In the *General Constitutions*, St. Ignatius promised the provinces an *ordo studiorum* for their colleges and universities. But, as Lukacs and Cosentino each observe, he was at pains to insist that, in their faithful observance of its directives, Jesuit educators should adapt them to person, place, and time. So it is no surprise to find that this spirit of calling on experience and adapting to circumstances all available resources, the *modus parisiensis* included, and then allowing rectors and professors discretion in the implementation of established *Ratio* directives, pervaded the thinking of the Congregations and committees who drafted the document; the administrators and teachers whose mission it was to implement the *Ratio* inherited the same Ignatian spirit from them.

Ignatian-obedient discretion became a Jesuit educational tradition, despite the inclination to impose a rigid uniformity that Lukacs noted in some key Jesuit officials. Tension between conformity and free-ranging experimentation in teaching mathematics no less than theology continued to test that Ignatian spirit up to the Suppression. After the Restoration of the Society in 1814, the *Ratio* continued to regulate Jesuit schools, though far less effectively for lack of adaptation of its Renaissance curriculum to new intellectual and social realities. The restored Society, still in shock and disarray from its dispersion, was cautious and conservative in its thinking. Unlike the Society of Ignatius, Nadal, and Bellarmine, it did not have the courage to be open to contemporary experience. Its recovery was slow and painful.

But it did recover. In nineteenth-century North America, still a missionary frontier, Jesuit schools were opened to help European immigrants enter the mainstream of American life. The strength of that educational apostolate, however, lay at the secondary school level. Not until the second half of the twentieth century were there any distinguished Jesuit college undergraduate programs. Graduate school programs, with rare exception, were dismally mediocre. Only when secular external academic associations set standards for accreditation, were the Jesuit schools moved to review their curricula, expand library and laboratory facilities, recruit qualified faculty, and revitalize their intellectual apostolate.

The Society's 31st General Congregation, convened at Rome in 1965, promulgated several incisive decrees about Jesuit education and the intellectual apostolate. Most notable were Decree 28 ("The Apostolate of Education"), Decree 29 ("Scholarly Work and Research"), and Decree 30 ("Cultivating the Arts in the Society [of Jesus]"). Here was a summons to dedicated excellence the modern Society and American Jesuits needed very much to hear, a call to renewal of work for the Church that had once been a distinguished part of Jesuit history, as Cosentino and Lukacs later reminded us. The Congregation drew attention to documents of the early Society written when the *Ratio* was being formulated, in particular to the recommendations of Clavius that looked to the promotion of mathematical sciences in the Society as a means of helping the Church in its work of inculturation. Cited also was the "Ordination on Training Mathematics Teachers" drafted by Bellarmine in 1593, and promulgated by Father General Acquaviva.

Significantly, the 34th General Congregation challenged Jesuits today to maintain and deepen the tradition, as the contributors to *Promise Renewed* make efforts to do in their individual disciplines. If Acquaviva's *Ratio studiorum* no longer governs schools once founded by Jesuits, the underlying Ignatian spirit of principled accommodation in service to the Catholic faith is alive and well in many of their corridors, as the pages of *Promise Renewed* amply testify.

BIBLIOGRAPHICAL NOTES

A modern critical edition of the 1599 *Ratio studiorum* is printed in *Monumenta Paedagogica Societatis Iesu, tom. V*, L. Lukacs, ed. (Roma: Institutum Historicum Societatis Iesu, 1986). No complete English translation of this annotated critical text is presently available. But see the planographed edition *The Jesuit Ratio Studiorum of 1599, translated into English with an introduction and explanatory notes by Allan P. Farrell* (Washington, D.C.: Conference of Major Superiors of Jesuits, 1970).

The bibliographical references already given suggest the wealth of studies relevant to the early Jesuit tradition in the mathematical sciences and to the history of the writing of the *Ratio studiorum*. Although it is not feasible to list here a complete bibliography even of English titles, it is useful to annotate, under three categories, some recent key references, especially European ones, that suggest the importance and place of the Lukacs and Cosentino papers in active historical research programs, and the considerable interest as well in Pre-Suppression Jesuit schools shown by general historians of mathematics and culture. Systematic bibliography compilation can well begin with the *Bibliographicus Conspectus* published yearly in *Archivum Historicum Societatis Iesu* (AHSI), which lists entries according to individual Jesuit names, e.g., Clavius, countries, and topics, such as the history of the *Ratio studiorum*. The concise bibliographical entries in the quarterly journal *Historia Mathematica* are by author and title, with key content words appended.

CONTEXTUAL STUDIES

Coyne, George V., S.J., M. A. Hoskin and O. Pedersen. *Gregorian Reform of the Calendar. Proceedings of the Vatican Conference to Commemorate its 400th Anniversary, 1582-1982* (Vatican City: Pontificia Academia Scientiarum/Specola Vaticana, 1983). Part IV (pp. 137-169) has Ugo Baldini's paper "Christopher Clavius and the Scientific Scene in Rome." Baldini evaluates mathematical activity at the Collegio Romano prior to 1582, and the technical nature of Clavius' work in astronomy and mathematics that won him a position on the Church's Calendar Reform Committee.

Dear, Peter R. *Discipline and Experience: The Mathematical Way in the Scientific Revolution* (Chicago: University of Chicago Press, 1995). Chapter 2 ("Experience and Jesuit Mathematical Science: The Practical Importance of Methodology") explains how Jesuit academic culture after the 1599 publication of the *Ratio* "included a place for mathematical sciences that involved a unique methodological conceptualization of the place of experience in the making of scientific knowledge." Clavius, Blancanus et al. worked to establish mathematics as a science in the Aristotelian sense, the issue that was at the center of the *De certitudine* controversy, and to link mathematics with physics (natural philosophy) to generate knowledge of the real world.

Farrell, Allan P., S.J. *The Jesuit Code of Liberal Education: Development and Scope of the Ratio Studiorum* (Milwaukee: Bruce, 1938). An old, but still valuable treatment, and the last major study of the *Ratio* by an American Jesuit.

Ganss, George E., S.J. *The Constitutions of the Society of Jesus: Translated with an Introduction and a Commentary* (St. Louis: Institute of Jesuit Sources, 1970). An approved translation of the official Latin text prior to its revision mandated by the Society's 34th General Congregation (for which see infra J.W. Padberg, S.J.).

The Spiritual Exercises of Saint Ignatius: A Translation and Commentary (St. Louis: Institute of Jesuit Sources, 1992). The celebrated text that is the foundation of the Society of Jesus and Jesuit apostolic life.

Grant, Edward. "In Defense of the Earth's Centrality and Immobility: Scholastic Reaction to Copernicanism in the Seventeenth Century," *Transactions of the American Philosophical Society*, n.s., 74 (1984), pt. 4. Grant examines the work of J. B. Riccioli and other Jesuit astronomers and mathematicians done in support of the Church's 1633 decision to put Copernicus on the Index of Forbidden Books. Their best contribution was a perceptive critique of gaps and errors in the logic of the Copernicans which forced them to improve their texts. The Jesuit scientists, who were trained in Clavius' Roman College Mathematics Academy and his doctrine of astronomical realism, were themselves constrained from developing heliocentric astronomy, and their efforts to refine the Ptolemaic system or Tycho Brahe's variant became increasingly futile. Advances in observational astronomy and the publication of Isaac Newton's *Principia Mathematica* ultimately made their attempts to defend Aristotelian physics, Ptolemaic astronomy, and the Church's condemnation of Copernicus and Galileo utterly hopeless, as Roger Boscovich, Clavius' eighteenth-century successor in the Roman College chair of mathematics, saw so clearly.

Heilbron, John L. *Elements of Early Modern Physics* (Berkeley: University of California Press, 1982). Heilbron indicates how in the seventeenth century the Catholic Church was the largest institutional patron of experimental natural philosophy (physics), and how within this structure the Jesuit order was the single most important contributor. According to his reading of Society archives, Jesuits inclined to Copernican astronomy and experimental physics often felt more comfortable working, with the blessing of Superiors, in the provinces away from the suspicious eyes of the Roman College Aristotelian establishment and the Inquisition.

Krayer, Albert. *Mathematik im Studienplan der Jesuiten: Die Vorlesung von Otto Catenius an der Universitat Mainz (1610-1611)* (*Mathematics in the Jesuit Ratio Studiorum: Otto Cattenius' Lectures at the University of Mainz [1610-1611]*) (Stuttgart: Franz Steiner Verlag, 1991). This specialized study of the mathematical lectures downplays Clavius' influence on the institutional teaching of mathematics, controverting earlier more positive estimates by Francois de Dainville, S.J., and others. Krayer notes the

11

consequences of the sharp disciplinary boundary the Aristotelian Jesuit philosophers established between mathematics and natural philosophy (physics) and then built into the Jesuit curriculum.

Lattis, James M. *Between Copernicus and Galileo: Christoph Clavius and the Collapse of Ptolemaic Cosmology* (Chicago: University of Chicago Press, 1994). Based on Lattis' 1989 University of Wisconsin doctoral dissertation, the book provides a badly needed biography of Clavius, as well as a detailed study of Clavius' monumental commentary on the *Sphere of Sacrobosco,* a medieval text of Ptolemaic astronomy. Clavius' commentary was used during his tenure as mathematics professor at the Roman College, and apparently also by Galileo in his early years of teaching at the University of Pisa. It had several editions, and remained a standard text well into the seventeenth century.

Moss, Joan D. *Novelties in the Heavens: Rhetoric and Science in the Copernican Controversy* (Chicago: University of Chicago Press, 1993). Moss' account of Galileo's newly found use of rhetoric in promoting heliocentrism considers the Roman College *ratio studiorum* and the mindset of the Jesuits trained there, Orazio Grassi, Christopher Grienberger, et al., who disputed with Galileo.

Padberg, John W., S.J., gen. ed. *The Constitutions of the Society of Jesus and Their Complementary Norms. A Complete English Translation of the Official Latin Texts* (St. Louis: Institute of Jesuit Sources, 1996). The 33d General Congregation mandated a revision of the *General Constitutions* and Society law in keeping with the new Code of Canon Law following Vatican Council II. The 34th General Congregation promulgated the revisions and the *Complementary Norms.*

Spence, Jonathan D. *The Memory Palace of Matteo Ricci* (New York: Viking Press, 1984). Spence, professor of Chinese History at Yale University, analyzes how Ricci used astronomy and the geometry of Euclid's *Elements* that he learned from Clavius at the Roman College for apostolic purposes at the Emperor's Court in Beijing. Ricci appealed to the Roman College for textbooks and Jesuit astronomer-mathematicians to follow up his own work of inculturation of the Gospel in China. Fathers Adam Schall van Bell and Ferdinand Verbiest were among those missioned there.

Wallace, William A., O.P., *Galileo and His Sources: The Heritage of the Collegio Romano in Galileo's Science* (Princeton: Princeton University Press, 1984). An exhaustively researched detection of

Galileo's early professorial use of lecture notes written by Roman College professors in the late 1580s, along with a description of educational practice in the College at the time of the development of the *Ratio*. After the demise in 1612 of his mathematical colleague Clavius, Galileo fell out with the Roman College Jesuits, and the bitter controversies over sun spots and heliocentrism ensued.

THE *DE CERTITUDINE MATHEMATICARUM* CONTROVERSY

Extensive research subsequent to Gilbert's 1960 monograph and Cosentino's 1970 paper has shed considerable light on the *De certitudine* controversy, and on the interplay between the evolving intellectual culture and the teachers in the new Jesuit educational apostolate. A notable instance where the controversy figures large is the magisterial study of Professor Paul Lawrence Rose: *The Italian Renaissance of Mathematics: Studies on Humanists and Mathematicians from Petrarch to Galileo* (Geneva: Droz, 1975). Subsequently, Oxford professor Alisdair C. Crombie examined the dispute in his note "Mathematics and Platonism in Sixteenth-Century Italian Universities and in Jesuit Educational Policy" that appeared in *PRISMATA: Naturwissenschaftsgeschictliche Studien [Festschrift für Willy Hartner]*, Y. Maeyama and W. G. Salzer, eds. (Wiesbaden: Franz Steiner Verlag, 1977), pp. 63-94. Frederick A. Homann, S.J., set the debate in terms of Clavius' celebrated 1574 text *Commentary on Euclid's Elements* in "Christopher Clavius and the Renaissance of Euclidean Geometry," AHSI 52 (1983), pp. 233-36.

G. C. Giacobbe studied individual disputants in papers from 1972 onwards. Two are especially pertinent: "Epigoni nel seicento della 'Quaestio de certitudine mathematicarum': Giuseppe Biancani," *Physis* 18 (1976), pp. 5-40, and "Un gesuita progressista nella 'Quaestio de certitudine mathematicarum': Benito Pereyra," *Physis* 19 (1977), pp. 51-86. Additional data on Biancani (Blancanus) can be found in the collection of papers by Ugo Baldini, *Legem impone subactis: Studi su filosophia e scienza dei gesuiti in Italia 1540-1632 (Legem impone subactis: Studies in the Philosophy and Science of Jesuits in Italy 1540-1632)* (Rome: Bulzoni, 1992), ch. 6, and passim. (An English translation has been announced by the University of Chicago Press.) Pereyra (Pereira), Clavius' Roman College antagonist, figures in the recent comprehensive treatment of Professor Anna De Pace, *Le matematiche e il mondo: Richerche su un dibattito in Italia nella seconda meta del Cinquecento (Mathematics and the World: Studies on a Debate in Italy in the Second Half of the Sixteenth Century)* (Milan: Francoangeli, 1993).

JESUIT COLLEGE MATHEMATICS PROGRAMS

Cosentino's next paper in the Domus Galileana Institute's program, "L'Insegnamento delle matematiche nei collegi gesuitici nell'Italia settentrionale: Nota introduttiva" ("Mathematics Instruction in Jesuit Colleges of Northern Italy. Introductory Note"), *Physis* 13 (1971), pp. 205-17 (English translation: this volume, pp. 81-95), emphasized the need to study the actual teaching of mathematics in Jesuit colleges, especially Italian ones, during and after the development of the *Ratio*. He listed briefly some available resources that can illustrate the effects of implementing the *Ratio* in the seventeenth century. These are found most of all in Society province catalog lists of members according to house and assignment, and in individual college or house diaries, but also in the school text books and research papers that Jesuit mathematical scientists produced. That they took up mathematics enthusiastically admits no doubt. Perusal of the *Dictionary of Scientific Biography* (C.C. Gillespie, ed., New York: Van Nostrand, 1974 et seq.) shows that by 1650 twenty-seven Jesuits had achieved appropriate scientific eminence to merit entry there. Sixteen were professors of mathematics; seven more at other posts wrote on the mathematical sciences.

Karl A. F. Fischer soon followed up Cosentino's lead, and cataloged Jesuit mathematicians in the German, French, and Italian Assistancies of the Society up to the 1762 Suppression in France, and 1773 elsewhere: "Jesuiten Mathematiker in der deutschen Assistanz bis 1773," AHSI 47 (1978), pp. 159-224, and "Jesuiten Mathematiker in der franzosischen und italienischen Assistanz bis 1762 bzw. 1773," AHSI 52 (1983), pp. 52-92. This complemented the work of François de Dainville, S.J., "L'Enseignement des mathématiques dans les collèges jésuites de France du XVIe au XVIIIe siècle," *Revue d'histoire des sciences et de leurs applications* 7, nn. 1-2 (1954), pp. 6-21, 102-23. Similarly, Father Omer van der Vyver, S.J., considered Gregory of St. Vincent and the distinguished Antwerp school of Jesuit geometers that had its roots in Clavius' Roman College mathematics academy: "L'École de mathématiques des Jésuites de la province Flandro-Belge au XVIIIe siècle," AHSI 49 (1980), pp. 265-78.

More localized is the study of R. Gatto, *Tra Scienza e Immaginazione: Le Matematiche Presso il Collegio Gesuitico Napoletano [1552-1670 ca.] (Between Science and Poetry: Mathematics in the Jesuit College of Naples [1552-c.1670])* (Florence: Olschki, 1994). Cf. also Steven J. Harris, "Les chaires de mathematiques," in *Les Jésuites à la Renaissance*, L. Giard, ed.

(Paris: Presses Universitaires de France, 1995), pp. 239-61, and "Transposing the Merton Thesis: Apostolic Spirituality and the Establishment of the Jesuit Scientific Tradition," *Science in Context* 3 (1989), pp. 29-65.

THE ENCOUNTER BETWEEN CATHOLICISM AND SCIENCE

Crucial as they were for the Society's apostolate of intellectual inculturation, implementation of the *Ratio studiorum*, academic freedom for Jesuit theologians, and decisions about the role of mathematics in the Jesuit curriculum, all inevitably figured in the spread of Copernicanism and the condemnation of Galileo. Today the amount of literature on the topic is experiencing exponential growth. Good examples are the papers from a 1981 international conference held at the University of Wisconsin, Madison, that are printed in *God and Nature: Historical Essays on the Encounter between Christianity and Science,* David C. Lindberg and Ronald L. Numbers, eds. (Berkeley: University of California Press, 1986). Of special interest for Jesuit studies are Robert S. Westman, "Copernicans and the Church," pp. 76-113, and William B. Ashworth, Jr., "Catholicism and Early Modern Science," pp. 136-66.

Valuable too is *The Cambridge Companion to Galileo,* Peter K. Machamer, ed. (New York: Cambridge University Press, 1998). See especially Rivka Feldhay, "The Use and Abuse of Mathematical Entities: Galileo and the Jesuits Revisited," ch. 3, pp. 80-145, that takes up questions treated in the author's text *Galileo and the Church: Political Inquisition or Critical Dialogue?* (New York: Cambridge University Press, 1995). Feldhay first examined the wall of separation the Jesuit Aristotelians erected between mathematics and natural philosophy (physics), and the need to maintain it, in her essay "Knowledge and Salvation in Jesuit Culture," *Science in Context* 1 (1987), pp. 195-213. If the Jesuits' cultural orientation posited the *vita activa* at the center of their worldview, they also saw their educational enterprise as a kind of apostolic activity helping to achieve salvation. Nonetheless, from Feldkay's point of view of the history of Western science, the 1599 publication of the *Ratio studiorum* was the "lost moment" of the Jesuit educational program. Clavius' attempt to modify the Aristotelian-Thomistic principles of the organization of knowledge was thwarted. The language of conformity prevailed even though the text betrayed the historical possibility of a breakthrough to modernity, a possibility that remained largely unactualized.

A History of the *Ratio Studiorum*

Ladislaus Lukacs, S.J.

PART I.

THE ORIGIN AND PROGRESS
OF THE JESUIT ORDER OF STUDIES

CHAPTER 1.
THE START OF COLLEGES AND EXTERN MINISTRY

1. COLLEGES FOR JESUIT SCHOLASTICS

St. Ignatius and his first companions proposed to found a new apostolic religious order to meet the needs of the times. Preaching the faith in infidel lands and its defense against heresy everywhere became their top priority. The order wanted to recruit only mature men, learned and strong in the faith, but soon realized how few there were available. It became necessary to admit young men and assign them to houses near prestigious universities where they could learn the necessary disciplines, as other religious orders did. Jesuit houses, however, were not like those of other orders. They were completely independent, neither attached to nor incorporated into the universities. Although Jesuit scholastics alone were admitted to them, these houses, nevertheless, did not sponsor any special or general academic programs for the scholastics, who instead heard the university lectures. By 1544 there were seven of these houses or colleges, at Paris, Coimbra, Padua, Louvain, Cologne, Valencia, and Alcalá.

2. TEACHING MINISTRY STARTED

College practice was soon modified. First, Jesuits were quickly forced to drop the policy that "no lectures are to be held in the house." University lectures were few, prolix, and without appropriate student exercises. To avoid making the scholastics' studies unduly long, the Jesuits began to teach some disciplines in their own houses. At the same time, another innovation, perhaps of greater moment, occurred in India. In Goa, in 1542, the bishop arranged for two Jesuits to teach boys in his diocesan seminary to read and write, and elements of Latin as well. With this began a Jesuit educational ministry that was to evolve gloriously over the years. Though teaching was not expressly listed in the Society's *Formula Instituti*, it is appropriately counted among "works of charity," so that the innovation in no way deviated from the original spirit of the Institute (as some Jesuits later feared), but should only be seen as an apostolic development.

3. EXTERN SCHOOLS APPROVED

After these innovations nothing prevented St. Ignatius in 1548 from accepting endowments for houses in Gandia, Spain, and Messina, Italy, that sponsored public lectures. These were the first ones established for both Jesuits and externs. The Messina college enjoyed extraordinary importance, and not just as a new apostolate for instruction of youth. Its plan of studies, devised by Father Nadal *ad modum parisiensem,* "according to the model of Paris," reached out to the whole Society.

CHAPTER 2.
ORDER AND IMPLEMENTATION OF STUDIES

St. Ignatius and his successors contributed a great deal to the development of a program of studies. So prior to a history of the *Ratio studiorum* itself, a survey of what Father Acquaviva's predecessors accomplished is in order, along with a review of the more important preparatory documents and versions.

A. ACTS AND DECREES: 1541-1556

a. STUDIES FOR JESUIT SCHOLASTICS

Once St. Ignatius decided to admit young men who were to be educated in the appropriate disciplines, he had to determine an academic program for their formation.

1. *FUNDACIÓN DE COLLEGIO*

The basic norms of that academic program were sketched in the 1541 document *Fundación de Collegio,* Paragraph 13, insisted that the goal of studies in the Society was a supernatural, apostolic, and practical one: it was to instruct members in the sacred sciences they needed to evangelize effectively and to defend the faith. First needed was a solid foundation in "litterae humaniores." After that the men were to be thoroughly trained in philosophy and theology. The better students could be awarded academic degrees for more authoritative exercise of ministry. The program could be modified, with features added or removed to meet the needs of time, place, and persons, for the service of the Church. Not surprisingly, these basic norms recurred in almost all later decrees on studies.

2. Padua College constitutions

Written as it was for prospective college benefactors, *Fundación de Collegio* provided wise, even if jejune, norms. Academic house rectors needed a more explicit document on program implementation, which in 1545 St. Ignatius promised them. In September 1546, some scholastics sent from Rome to Padua, brought constitutions, written in Italian and adapted for use in that house. They were in four parts, the first part treating the program of studies. Its sixth paragraph specified the studies required, and, importantly, the student exercises, since St. Ignatius and his companions admired the Parisian colleges, and proposed them as models in the *General Constitutions*.

3. Polanco's *Industriae* and *Constitutiones Collegiorum* (1547-1550)

In 1547 St. Ignatius called Father Polanco to Rome from Padua, where that year he had completed his studies, to assist him with the *General Constitutions*. The project began to move well, and St. Ignatius could not have found a more industrious and docile aide. But because the writing took more time than allowed for an early mailing to the provinces, St. Ignatius instructed Polanco to draft an instruction for the interim regulation of the scholastics' formation and literary studies.

Polanco responded with two valuable documents, the *Industriae* and the *Constitutiones Collegiorum*. Both listed study topics important for scholastics, and gave new norms for their admission to studies. *Fundación* considered only the scholastics destined for literary, philosophical, or theological studies. *Industriae*, on the other hand, divided the scholastics into two groups: those giving promise of academic excellence, and the others. The first group were to study philosophy and theology in depth, the second, not so much. *Constitutiones Collegiorum*, in turn, classified scholastics as "distinguished" or "mediocre," and barred the latter from the study of philosophy or theology. This norm found its way into the *General Constitutions*.

4. SCHOLASTIC STUDIES IN THE *GENERAL CONSTITUTIONS*

Although St. Ignatius promised them constitutions, and for that reason the colleges very much wanted them, much to everyone's surprise, the *Constitutiones Collegiorum* were never sent to the colleges, even after Polanco's careful revision. Perhaps the principal reason was that in 1550 the oldest text of the *General Constitutions* had already been written, and St. Ignatius aimed to promulgate it soon. Also, there was by that time a new kind of college, one that had lectures open to all. In composing *Constitutiones Collegiorum* Polanco had in mind only colleges designed for instruction of Jesuits. New colleges had been opened in 1546 at Gandia, and in 1548 at Messina, and because of the large number of extern students enrolled, they needed different constitutions and rules.

That the *Industriae* and *Constitutiones Collegiorum* really achieved Polanco's goal is clear since their provisions made their way into the *General Constitutions*. Their topics are common: how to find candidates for the Society, their requisite qualities, how to foster their spiritual growth and physical health, instruction in doctrine and letters, preparing them for fruitful apostolic ministry and assignment in the Lord's vineyard once they have finished studies, and, finally, the governance and preservation of the Society.

b. STUDIES IN JESUIT SCHOOLS FOR EXTERNS

When a new college with public lectures was started at Messina in 1548, Father Jerome Nadal, the college rector, asked for a directive, or constitutions for supervision of its lecture program. Father Orviedo, the rector at Gandia, did likewise. St. Ignatius in turn asked both to compose directives and to submit them to Rome for approbation.

1. UNIVERSITY OF GANDIA STATUTES (1549-1550)

Father Araoz, the Spanish provincial, Father Miron, the rector at Valencia, and Father Rojas, the superior at Zaragoza, all collaborated with Orviedo to draft statutes based for the most part on the University of Valencia constitutions, but adapted *ad modum parisiensem*. What they wrote, however, did not treat pedagogical practice, but almost only examination methods and the conferral of academic degrees.

2. THE MESSINA CONSTITUTIONS (1548)

At Messina, Nadal also finished work in 1548. His text, looking only to public lectures and extern students, had two sections. The first gave general principles and methods of fostering devotion in young students.

The other section outlined lecture schedules and the distribution of studies: the various classes of grammar and literary studies, Greek and Hebrew, philosophy and mathematics, and then scholastic theology and Sacred Scripture. Casuistry classes and some scholastic exercises were also included. His Messina constitutions were harbingers of all subsequent study programs, and for this reason their influence on the *Ratio studiorum* is all the more pervasive. In 1549 Nadal transcribed them for use of a new college at Palermo. When this news reached Spain, Aroaz wrote for a copy. St. Ignatius, too, wanted the Messina constitutions submitted to the scrutiny of the Jesuits he had summoned to Rome in 1550 to study the *General Constitutions,* and on their approval, sent to the other Jesuit colleges. When the Society started public lectures in Rome in 1551, St. Ignatius thought to model Roman practice after that of Messina. So Nadal took pains to describe the Medina practice and reported it to Rome, whence it was soon widely diffused. The *modus messanensis* became a resource for the whole Society, and the Messina college the prototype of all the Society's extern colleges.

3. The *Modus Parisiensis* Model

To Nadal's credit, he adapted to the Society's purposes at Messina, and there implemented, the *modus parisiensis* that early Jesuits thought so far superior to the *modus italicus.* In Paris the faculty was then dominant in the university; in Italy, the student body. Lectures were held in university affiliated colleges in Paris; in Italy, in the university itself. Paris had effective student supervision; Italy allowed students great freedom. A carefully determined curriculum bound professor and student alike in Paris, with frequent professorial lectures followed by appropriate student exercises. Distinct groups were designated, and students enrolled by academic discipline. Each class had its proper professor and syllabus. Students were promoted only after careful examination. Students and instructors were close: the professor could monitor a student's progress. The Society prized these features of the *modus parisiensis* above what the *modus italicus* offered. Young persons progressed better and faster in the Parisian system.

4. The Roman College: *Alma Mater* of all Jesuit Colleges

From its very beginning the Roman College played a special role in Jesuit education. St. Ignatius saw it as the source of Society teachers: "From the Roman College, like a spring, to quote Father Ledesma (its first dean), there should emanate teachers, and schools, and faculties for other places. Men should be fostered and trained here, so they can teach and share the good things the College has given them." And so, even in St. Ignatius' lifetime, instructions for Jesuits missioned to new educational apostolates often insisted that they take Roman College practice as their model for studies and academic procedure. The rules Polanco wrote in 1551 for the rector of the Roman College were immediately sent to the provinces, and the *Constitutions* recommended their use.

5. UNIVERSITY STUDIES IN THE *CONSTITUTIONS*

Promotion of the Gandia and Messina programs to university level moved St. Ignatius to think of preparing an order of general studies, i.e., university level work. Such a plan had already been promised for both colleges and universities in the oldest text of the *Constitutions*, written in 1547-1550. However, nothing of the sort is found in the earlier or second text of the *Constitutions*. Only at the end of 1553, or early 1554, were the seven chapters dealing with universities written by St. Ignatius and inserted after the ten chapters of the Fourth Part of the *Constitutions*. He wanted to learn the right path from experts and experience. So he decreed that the Gandia and Messina rectors should develop guidelines and follow them "until the Superior General legislate[s] for all the universities." He asked the Gandia rector to study the constitutions of the universities at Valencia, Alcalá, Salamanca, and Coimbra, and to forward them to Rome. He wanted copies of the constitutions of the universities at Paris, Louvain, Cologne, Bologne, and Padua, "to see what other universities do, how to improve our procedures, how they write general constitutions, and how this could serve the Society's universities and colleges." Documents of Fathers Olave and Nadal, both seasoned educators, also proved useful: Olave's *Order of Lectures and Exercises Followed in the Jesuit University*, and Nadal's *Order and Arrangement of the Studium Generale*. Only after he studied their texts did St. Ignatius write, with Polanco's help, the university chapters that prescribed the disciplines to be taught, their order and method, the books used, curricula and academic degrees, the religious life of the students, and university administration. Although they touched all basic and necessary matters, the chapters were juridical in nature, and said little about program implementation. The *Constitutions*, however, promised full treatment of these topics elsewhere.

B. Program Difficulties: 1557–1580

1. The Roman College *Ratio Studiorum* (1558)

Successors to St. Ignatius did not overlook his promise of a program of studies. The obligation fell most of all to the Roman College whose professors, mindful of it and at the behest of superiors, in 1557 summarized their class orders and pedagogical methods. They drafted at the same time a new *ratio studiorum* for the College that members of the First General Congregation (1558) copied for use in their own schools. Yet its traces were so completely erased that it was no simple matter even to prove its existence or locate a copy. Although quite brief, and sketchy in parts, that Roman College *Ratio* foreshadowed later formulations. For along with the order of classes there were rules for the prefect of studies, the teachers, and the students. Father Nadal, Visitor to the German Assistancy in 1562, adapted it to the situation there. He elaborated the order of classes, and amplified the rules for the prefect of studies. Northern Jesuit schools were held to this Ordo until 1570, when Rome sent the first *Ratio studiorum,* prepared at Father General Borgia's request, and promulgated in his name for the whole Society.

2. Borgia's *Ratio Studiorum* (1565-1572)

In 1563/4 the Roman College met at length to evaluate its study program. Father Ledesma, College prefect and chairman of the sessions, meticulously informed Father General Laínez about the proceedings, and proposed action, recommending "that there be a book to contain explicitly and in detail the complete program of studies, both for this and for the other colleges that have grammar classes, or lectures in other faculties, and that the program be described explicitly and specifically for each class and faculty, for each office and operation, for academic acts, disputations, and literary exercises; and that with the discerning judgment of superiors, it be implemented, with no changes whatever, unless made by the highest council of the Society, so that at last we have a definite program that the prefect of studies and the professors must follow."

Father Laínez, St. Ignatius' immediate successor, on his return from Trent to Rome in early 1564, told the Roman College professors to draft such a *ratio studiorum.* Neither the sudden death of Laínez in January 1565, nor the subsequent General Congregation delayed their work, so that by the end of 1565 the part treating "litterae humaniores" was already completed. A commission then revised it, and at the end of 1569 it was distributed to the provinces. The first common, comprehensive *ratio studiorum*, it was promulgated by order and authority of Father General Francis Borgia, and appropriately called Borgia's *Ratio studiorum*. The document's importance comes from its use until 1591 when the Society received the temporary *Ratio studiorum* of Father General Claude Acquaviva. Borgia allowed local superiors considerable leeway in implementing his *Ratio*. Its preface echoed the *Constitutions*: "Everything prescribed here must be adapted to place, time, and persons, although the program should be observed as much as possible."

Borgia had rules for the prefect of studies, preceptors, Jesuit scholastics, extern students, and the corrector or beadle. A long essay followed the rules, listing the grades of each class, the disciplines taught, miscellaneous exercises, examinations, and schedules. Although Borgia's *Ratio* foreshadowed the final form of the Jesuit program, Ledesma, who got the text for criticism, nevertheless thought it was inadequate. True, it specified what, where, when, and by whom things were to happen in the school, but it did not explain how all that was to be done. His remarks are of interest to teachers: "I don't think it is sufficient to prescribe a program of studies in vague and general terms. It should specify for each class and exercise the best plan and method for the instructor to follow." Yet not even the definitive 1599 *Ratio studiorum* escaped the defect Ledesma bemoaned.

At this same time Rome developed both a *ratio* for "litterae humaniores" and one for philosophy (*De artium liberalium studiis*), and they were sent at least to a few provinces. There is, however, no evidence that the provinces also received a theological section *(De sacrae theologiae studiis)*. We know only that the Roman College experimented with it.

3. LIBERTAS OPINANDI AND DELECTUS OPINIONUM

In 1571 the part of Borgia's *Ratio* that treated scholastic philosophy was ready to be sent to the provinces. Nevertheless that did not happen before Borgia's death the next year. Not surprisingly, the provinces in 1573 petitioned the General Congregation to get this important part finished and promulgated. The Roman province congregation, for example, wrote that "Experience shows the great advantage in keeping all possible uniformity in theology and philosophy, so far as circumstances allow, and in the teaching methods of our Society's colleges as well. We ask the General Congregation that a common Formula be imposed, or that some method, developed carefully at Rome and taking into account others' opinions, be drafted and given official sanction." Father Edward

Mercurian, the new General, reported that "Uniformity and method in philosophy and theology have been carefully studied here at Rome. The work done will be sent first to the provinces for their comments.... After that, a *ratio studiorum* can be prescribed with confidence for the Society."

Father General's wish to hear the whole Society before deciding this complex and difficult matter is something quite new. Yet during Mercurian's generalate there was neither consultation of the whole Society nor was the scholastic theology part of Borgia's *Ratio* distributed. In 1579, shortly before his death, Mercurian replied to the Peruvian congregation that "With the divine help, it will soon be promulgated." The chief, if not only cause of the long delay arose in the Roman College where once again bitter controversies raged about freedom of choice in speculative theology.

The problem first arose there when Laínez was General, and later elsewhere. Because there was no officially sanctioned theological author, each professor chose his own doctrine. A grave crisis arose for the unity of the Society's teaching. The Roman province congregation in 1568 openly faced the danger: "The greatest cause of ignorance and confusion is that solid doctrine is not explained in the liberal arts curriculum, but instead young and inexperienced instructors develop their own doctrine." Two values clashed: doctrinal orthodoxy and professorial freedom in research. Controversy here could undermine union of minds and hearts. And so Jesuits often asked professors not to introduce new doctrines without the permission of superiors. Fear and aversion to anything new intensified the struggle for many of them.

Father Toledo was the first Roman College theologian criticized by other Jesuits for his views on predestination. In 1561, however, he recurred to Laínez, then at the Council of Trent, who did not force him to revise the opinions that had been challenged. The question was open, and the Church had defined nothing to the contrary, so that Father General could reply that "The Society should not prescribe particular opinions (as on predestination) so rigorously as to condemn others, weaken charity, or give scandal." Father Benedict Peirera was severely castigated, especially by Ledesma and Gagliardi, for his philosophical Averroism. Bitter controversy broke out in the upper German province about doctrinal orthodoxy. Father Pisa, a Spaniard, was accused of fostering new opinions. The provincial, Father Hoffaeus, on mandate of Father General, was obliged to write an extensive directive about obligatory doctrine to effect a troubled peace among the Jesuits. Another distinguished professor in the province, Gregory of Valencia, honored for defense of the Catholic faith there in Germany, was denounced as unorthodox, and Hoffaeus had to defend him to the General. Even the preeminent Jesuit theologian Suárez stood accused of the crime of innovation. In a letter to the General in 1579, he protested his innocence of the fault, and indicated how he held common positions, and in methodology differed only insignificantly from common practice.

Hoffaeus knew how difficult it was for theologians to work amid rabid demands for doctrinal uniformity. In 1578 he proposed to Father General that "in speculative matters, where one can make a choice without danger to the faith or scandalizing others, professors should be accorded genuine freedom, for if we squeeze their brains too much, we may draw blood." Father General's response supported Hoffaeus's paternal benevolence "within reason," noting that "it seems a good idea that their work is not so restricted, and that they be given some space; I approve, but within reason *(intra modum)*. Be careful when you let them move and work in so many directions that they don't imprison themselves in abstruse and inaccessible topics from which they can't extricate themselves." Nadal had a wise solution to the problem: according to his norm, the Portuguese professors could study probable opinions privately, but in public lectures they should profess more certain and approved doctrine, as the Society's *Constitutions* prescribed.

In theology the clash between doctrinal certainty and intellectual freedom is fraught with great danger, since here faith is at risk. Ledesma, who tried everything to restrict freedom, was the first Jesuit to compile a list of theses that professors had to teach. In 1564 he wrote to Father General: "Among the opinions that touch the faith, let the professors defend those we have listed on a separate sheet, and let them oppose their contraries." Father General Borgia, promptly adopting Ledesma's position on obligatory questions, published in 1565 a decree "Theses that are to be taught and defended in philosophy and theology," the first document of its kind in the Society. Ledesma, its source and guiding light, upheld it vigorously, even after Borgia's death. In a 1574 memorandum to Father Mercurian, the new General, he argued at length that "it is not only forbidden to teach anything against or even less consistent with the faith, but even more, certain specific opinions are banned; opinions that seem needed or useful to foster sound doctrine are mandated." Ledesma died the following year. He found in Father Tucci a worthy successor for defense of doctrinal orthodoxy. Tucci also compiled a list of theses which will be reviewed at the appropriate time.

Part II.

Preparation of the *Ratio Studiorum* 1581-1599

Chapter 1.

Results and Decisions: 1581-1582

A. The *Ratio Studiorum* and the Fourth General Congregation (1581)

After Father General Mercurian's death, the provinces wanted even more the *ratio studiorum* promised them. The Polish congregation spoke for the whole Society: "The congregation requests that this postulate be among those accepted: that Rome finally issue a *ratio studiorum* common to the whole Society as far as possible." A Neapolitan province postulate is also notable: "The congregation wishes the General Congregation to decide which philosophical and theological theses of those Reverend Father Borgia mandated, Ours are to hold in the future." Clearly, the question of intellectual freedom was not at all dormant, but a matter the General they were to elect was expected to handle forthrightly. Although the Fourth General Congregation established a special twelve man commission to "determine a *ratio studiorum*," yet because of many difficulties inherent in the program and lack of time, the committee accomplished little.

B. Consultations and the Decree of obligatory Society Doctrine (1582)

Father Acquaviva, the new General, thought the question of obligatory doctrine should be one of the first resolved. His response to the Neapolitan province reflected his priorities: "A complete *ratio studiorum* now in preparation will prescribe policy about theological options. In the meantime the provinces will get an instruction that explains procedures for unity and solidity of doctrine and opinion." His first statement also gives us some fresh data. Scholars commonly held that nothing had been done about a *ratio studiorum* from 1581 to 1583, when Acquaviva established a special commission. The revision is supported by a letter of Acquaviva in September 1582 with a directive about the doctrine Jesuit teachers were expected to profess: "A *ratio studiorum* is not yet complete, though work on it began after the general congregation." He directed Father Deca, a Spaniard and an eminent theology professor (who, as elector of his province, was a member of the general congregation's commission on studies), that on return to his province he should evaluate the doctrine of its professors.

Deca reported that "I never realized the importance of what Your Reverence asked of me about the doctrine of Ours until I came to Spain and this college. From the moment I set out for Rome I realized I could expect nothing else than that those who taught here would completely abandon St. Thomas were I to turn my back on the situation." As an effective remedy, he urged "nothing other than to return entirely to the doctrine of St. Thomas." He wrote an essay in support of the idea, and asked Acquaviva to send it to some experts for their opinion, which he did. Father Robert Bellarmine, in Rome, thought that Deca's proposal "to strike from St. Thomas' theses only the one about the Blessed Virgin Mary's Immaculate Conception, and to keep the others, doesn't seem to be a good idea, but a difficult (or even impossible) task, and quite unnecessary." But in the end he conceded that "St. Thomas should be chosen as the approved and common teacher, provided that some of his theses are omitted."

In 1582 Acquaviva also addressed Roman College professors about doctrine in the Society: "Are there any theses that should be proscribed, or others we should teach? Or would it suffice to set rules that regulate *prohibenda* and *praecipienda* in a general way?" Ledesma lobbied vigorously for the first option; the Roman College backed the other, though some teachers thought that to avoid scandal a few opinions should be proscribed. Two rules were needed: first, professors should not deviate from St. Thomas, save rarely and for serious cause. Second, if reputable scholars do not endorse an opinion, professors should consult the superior who will review the matter, and either allow or forbid its teaching.

Acquaviva chose also to consult Father Salmerón, then in Naples, because of his reputation in theology. To his question "what *ratio studiorum* should we follow for philosophy and theology?," Salmerón replied that he saw little advantage for the Society to choose a specific doctor as its guide, and to bind all Jesuits to his text and theses. True, St. Thomas was a distinguished theologian, and Ignatius wisely cited him as an author Jesuits should read in the university. Yet "should one of Ours, sent by God, explain theological doctrine from a new perspective and with greater intelligibility, as was Blessed Ignatius' hope, then he should not be impeded, but the whole matter referred to Father General." Salmerón vetoed any list of prescribed theses for Jesuit professors since "the results were not happy whenever it was tried before." The Society should try however to have its professors limited to what Sacred Scripture and the Church teach.

The last Jesuit Acquaviva consulted about Society doctrine was Father Maldonato, elected by the French province as a member of the Fourth General Congregation. Maldonato thought the matter "of such great moment that it is neither possible nor desirable to resolve it in a short time." For now, some people should collect all the arguments for both sides, and others record less promising ideas. They should spend considerable time before they decide "what can be defended as probable, but as less probable than the contrary, and what cannot be defended even as probable." Finally, "there should in the meantime be a forum for new ideas, once these few rules we have been debating are sent to the provinces."

Acquaviva agreed that the question of doctrinal regulation could not be resolved in a short time. He also took the advice that while a plan for higher studies was being readied, he himself should promulgate rules for studies, and in September 1582 issued six norms about teaching the doctrine of St. Thomas. Maldonato was kept at Rome after the general congregation, not as theology teacher in the Roman College (Suárez had already been called to Rome for that purpose), but to supervise writing a *ratio studiorum*. At his premature death in early 1583, Father Tucci succeeded him in the task. According to the Faculty List, Tucci was a Roman College theology professor for the scholastic year 1581-1582. Afterwards he was not listed as a teacher, no doubt because he was preoccupied with drafting a *ratio studiorum*.

Chapter 2.
The 1586 *Ratio Studiorum*

A. The Commission drafts *Delectus Opinionum* and *Praxis et Ordo Studiorum* (1583-1586)

In early 1583 Father General determined to appoint a special committee to draft an *ordo studiorum*. He called to Rome experts "to draw up a single plan of studies to provide uniformity in speculative matters, as well as solid and useful doctrine. [The committee] should prescribe practical ways to treat the various sciences and faculties for the goal and development our Institute has set for itself."

The experts were in Rome by autumn 1583, and on 8 December the Holy Father received and blessed them as they began their work. First, they had to face the thorny question of choice of opinions *(de delectu opinionum)*. They examined each and every question of St. Thomas' *Summa Theologica,* and others about Scripture, Church, and Tradition not found there, but matter nonetheless for debate with heretics. How they did it, methodically and carefully, is recorded in the *Acta Congregationis.* The result was the *De delectu opinionum,* i.e., the propositions drawn from St. Thomas' *Summa,* both those the commission decided Jesuit professors should teach, and those they left optional. Though its text is missing, a great deal can be surmised from the *Iudicium* of the Roman College professors who studied it at Father General's request. Of course, this was not the *Delectus opinionum* that later appeared in the 1586 *Ratio studiorum,* but a provisional document with 597 required and optional propositions. The *Delectus opinionum* of the 1586 *Ratio* had a far fewer 126 propositions. The compilers of this first *Delectus* listed the propositions under such headings as Theology, Divine Simplicity, Predestination, etc., which were omitted in the 1586 *Ratio.* Accompanying the text was a *Commentary* where they explained why they classified theses as obligatory or optional. The Roman College reviewers mentioned this *Commentary* in their hypercritical *Iudicium* which totally rejected the text. Doctrinal solidity and unity of minds, its whole purpose, could hardly be achieved with a list of 597 theses. To impose that many propositions was "useless, and likely to cause grave problems both for teaching and for the peace and harmony of the Society; implementation will be at best difficult, and, more likely, impossible." Decisions should be made according to these criteria: theses that have no connection with religion or devotion, or are not concerned with grave matters, or are not the opinions of leading theologians, should not be mandated. The review board thought some committee theses false, and others indefensible and better proscribed than imposed; there was no reason for the inclusion of many others that were *de fide definita* or almost so. Still others seemed obscure or ambiguous; some optional theses were more important than ones that were mandated; there was no reason to include them rather than other optional ones. According to Bellarmine, "there are 77 theses in the collection that we think are against the mind of St. Thomas." Finally, the reviewers objected that although the 597 propositions of *Delectus opinionum* surveyed all theology, the result was not a coherent doctrinal corpus, but a "scattered and confused congeries of opinions." They examined only the propositions from the *Prima Pars* of the *Summa,* 130 of the entire 597, with the idea that a negative judgment here would be a clear message of what they thought about the whole thing.

Acquaviva told the Roman College to review *Praxis et Ordo Studiorum* as well as *De delectu opinionum,* but their report on it did not ask for extensive text revision. The committee's documents were ready and sent to him after August 1584, and the Roman College *Iudicium* submitted at the end of 1584 or early in 1585. However, as the *Acta Congregationis* noted, the General could not study them until the end of 1585. On review, he directed that *Praxis et Ordo Studiorum* be sent to the printer, but the speculative text had to be reconsidered, at least in part. There would be more profound revision at another time, after Rome received the provincial comments.

Three committee members in Rome, Tucci, Azor, and Gonzales, revised the 130 *Summa* propositions the Roman College faculty examined, so that this part could take its proper place ahead of the *Praxis et Ordo Studiorum* in the printed text of the *Ratio*. While it was in press, the committee and the professors met to review propositions drawn from other parts of the *Summa*. These could only appear as an appendix. This way the Society's first *Ratio studiorum* was promulgated and sent to the provinces in April 1586.

B. The 1586 printing of the *Ratio*

1. Remarks

Remarks are in order about the notable rarity of copies. First, few were made since the book was published as a manuscript "for greater ease in getting a generous supply of exemplars" out to the provinces. For the time being, colleges and schools did not get copies, but committees were appointed in each province to examine and evaluate the text. The Society had twenty provinces in 1586. If five copies were sent to each province, 100, or at most 120, copies would suffice. Very few have been preserved, to our knowledge, notably in Rome, Milan, London, Dublin, Berlin, and Treves. To explain this paucity, Sommervogel suggested that the exemplars were destroyed because Pope Sixtus V ordered a new and corrected edition. His sheer guess has no documentary basis. In fact, Sixtus used his authority to return to the Society the books intercepted by the Spanish Inquisition.

The real explanation is much simpler. The Aquataine province's report on the 1586 *Ratio* asked Father General that "When the entire *Ratio studiorum* has been finished, he order the provinces to burn all these exemplars." Acquaviva was of that mind. In a letter to the provinces that

31

accompanied the 1599 *Ratio studiorum* he ordered that "When Your Reverence receives this book, collect the old copies of the *Ratio* sent to the province, and burn them all. They have no further use. Make sure you do this."

2. THE AUTHORS' PURPOSE

Acquaviva explicitated the general aim in a letter of 24 August 1583 to the Austrian provincial: "We have decided, as many wish and the situation itself demands, to establish a study program that the Society can use from now on. This has been effected after mature and deliberate reflection, so that as far as possible, it shall admit no change or variation." His general principle was "to settle nothing until instructors in all provinces can give their opinions of the entire document." This way, "what was drafted for common use will have common support." The commission members hoped "that from the comments, reports, and criticisms received from the provinces, consensus could be had with greater confidence." And so they expected that "Once they knew practices and programs in the various countries, they could unanimously draft a program appropriate, as far as possible, for all of them." The commission paid close attention to the problem of mandatory Society teaching, explaining that "it has always seemed best if variation in teaching no less than intellectual freedom were constrained by law."

To evaluate this *Ratio* correctly, one must look at both the writers' intention and the nature of the project. The *Acta Congregationis* sheds light on the latter: "The six committee members explored what they thought would best effect the total study program." They produced papers and treatises, but not rules, statutes, or directions about the subjects to be taught. The treatises proposed program topics, theological, philosophical, and literary, for review by groups the provinces were to appoint. The committee evolved particular arguments so that "anything thought to touch the emendation or illustration of a specific item, is entered at that point, and everything can be seen coherently and at once by the reviewers." After that, "the corpus must be broken down into individual parts, i.e., into norms for students, professors, deans, rectors, provincials, et al."

3. THE SOURCES

The first *Ratio studiorum* reflected established practice and tradition. It was neither the task nor the goal of its authors to produce something new. They left copious references to their sources. According to the *Acta*

Congregationis: "To plan the disciplines and faculties to develop, they restudied the fourth section of the *Constitutions,* and tried to observe it diligently; the decrees of the congregations, the rules and statutes of the schools, and especially published Roman College customs and practices, were likewise reviewed. Attention was directed to the Roman College, as well as to other prestigious colleges and universities, both Jesuit and non-Jesuit." A bit later: "There was a review of the recorded deliberations on the matter, whether held at Rome or in the more notable Society colleges. Reports were analyzed, as were university decrees and laws, and other documents of similar nature, some earlier, others lately sent to Father General from Italy, Spain, France, Germany, and Poland.... From these many venerable practices were kept, some more recent ones adopted, and still others abrogated. If doubts arose, each member recounted the private or common practices in his province, the usages and precedents of the schools, their customs and results. We used these resources to meet many difficulties, and wholeheartedly agreed that nothing would be more useful for the schools, or our reputation and acceptance, than that all follow a single norm in developing talent and administering academic enterprises." (The sources are all reprinted in *Monumenta Paedagogica,* volumes I–IV.) In short, the commission diligently collected, studied, and chose the better things tradition and copious experience offered for a *ratio studiorum.*

4. PROVINCE RESPONSES

Acquaviva's letter of 21 April 1586 gave precise instructions about the province commissions and how they were to proceed. He hoped their responses could be sent to Rome by the end of 1586, and evaluated so that by the end of 1587 a new *Ratio* could be presented to the Procurators Congregation. Events turned out quite otherwise.

The *Ratio studiorum* text was sent out at the end of April 1586. Five provinces, Castile, Belgium, Aragon, Spain, and upper Germany, got the text in June, Austria and Milan in July, Poland in August, and France in September. Aquataine had not received it by October, and Campagne only in January 1587. By that time most of the other province comments were already in Rome. Only Castile's response was missing, never made because the Spanish Inquisition ordered the copies of the *Ratio studiorum* text impounded, and kept the Jesuits from examining it.

Chapter 3.
The Ratio Studiorum 1586B
(1587-1588)

A. The 1588 *Ratio Studiorum* text revised at Rome

Province comments came to Rome by the end of 1586. Although Tucci, Azor, and Gonzales began to study them right away, the attentive reading of almost 30 files needed about an entire year, as Tucci wrote to Acquaviva. Reading finished, they then drafted a new text, the *Ratio studiorum* 1586B, which, however, was never printed, or even sent to the provinces in manuscript form. It was in fact just an edited earlier text, and only a guide for a true *Ratio studiorum* complete with rules. For that reason it was forgotten until now. Its text appeared in two compact booklets, the first detailing higher studies, the other, preparatory classes. The front page of the first bore the title *De Scripturis*. A pre-Suppression Society archivist, seeing that title, and without further investigation thinking the book dealt entirely with Scripture, catalogued it as that. In the booklets, we find along with the Scripture treatise all the other disciplines that the 1586 *Ratio studiorum* treated. The two texts are however so different that the second is really a revised edition. Nor are they of the same length. The higher studies section was shortened, but the preparatory studies text underwent greater change. Some chapters were entirely new, others omitted. Acquaviva's letter to Father Maggio of 18 October 1587 noted that: "Although there was a demand that the procurators promulgate a study plan, that was not possible since a *new plan* had to be devised." Arrangement of material stayed fixed in *Ratio studiorum 1586B*, but the *Delectus opinionum* and its *Commentariolus* were dropped.

After the section on the importance of Scripture study, the editors added to the treatise an entirely new chapter, *Incitamenta studiorum Scripturarum*, that listed at length seven such motives. Completely redone were the first and third of the ten chapters in the scholastic theology section, treating the time for theology and the number of professors, and the lectures themselves, respectively. The rest were essentially unchanged. In *De humanioribus litteris*, the first chapter, separating the literature faculty from those of higher studies, was dropped. Chapters 5, 6, 8, 9, and 12 were completely new.

B. Preparation of a new *Delectus Opinionum*

Province reactions to the *Ratio studiorum* arrived in Rome. Father General, looking to a procurators congregation scheduled for the end of 1587, had asked the province congregations to recommend whether a general congregation should be convoked to approve the *Ratio studiorum*. Practically all said no, and for the same reason. The Roman province, for example, allowed that a general congregation could lend weight to an *ordo studiorum,* but that was not important enough to justify the inconvenience and work of convening the delegates. The project would need more time than was properly allotted a general congregation. The study program should first be implemented, and experience allowed to uncover any defects. After that, a general congregation could better and more surely confer its authority. That in fact happened with the 1593-1594 Fifth General Congregation.

The *Delectus opinionum* was written by a commission, rejected by the Roman College faculty, redone, and printed in the *Ratio studiorum*. Understandably, on being submitted to the provinces, it received adverse judgment, and the need for revision became even clearer. In 1588, Father Tucci, principal revision editor, went to Tusculum, by himself, to develop a new text. His long letter of 6 September to Father Acquaviva provides valuable data for the history of his revision. Tucci described his methodology in *Prefatio in duos propositionum catalogos* in the *Commentariolus* that discussed the optional propositions of the first part of the *Summa:* "Many propositions have an explanatory scholion to prevent the terseness useful for schematic listing from obscuring which ones are optional, and which not. Everything is explained clearly and distinctly, so that as far as can be, no one can think he is given a option when he is not, or that he is bound, when free. ... Each proposition has a scholion. So that theses do not seem proposed arbitrarily, the basics of all these topics are explained briefly, and the Church Doctors' argumentation transcribed *ad verbum.*" Finally, "It is important that the scholia have the same authority and weight as the propositions they elucidate. Yet they were developed not by deliberation of the whole Society, but by a single teacher, and not to obligate Ours, but to afford credible evidence that what is obligated, or left optional, can be supported, either definitively or arguably, and rests on good authority and reason; with this, no one can claim this thesis selection and evaluation is intellectual coercion."

C. THE *RATIO* AND THE HOLY OFFICE

The speculative part of the *Ratio* that Tucci completely redid, was submitted to Pope Sixtus V in late 1589 or early 1590, perhaps to forestall a new confrontation with the Spanish Inquisition. But difficulties remained after the Pope's death. Shortly thereafter it was submitted to Pope Gregory XIV, who asked the Cardinals of the Holy Office to evaluate it. The reader they appointed for that purpose wrote a report, preserved in Rome, in two parts: first, the *Pars speculativa* submitted by the Society, then his response. The *Pars speculativa* had Acquaviva's preface, a list of optional theses and an *animadversio*, plus a part on choice of opinions for professors of Scripture and Apologetics. The Holy Office did not receive the large set of treatises and commentaries on the rules, or the scholia for the *List of Theses*. Remarkably, also missing were the rules for choice of opinions.

The reader's response began: "The Jesuits ask whether it is appropriate to fix a book of theses from St. Thomas, so that their teachers would be held to scholastic doctrine, especially that of St. Thomas, and that scholars and students would not have the option, as is now the case, to range widely in doctrinal matters (which seems to be done with great harm), nor would there be any ambiguity, and all would know clearly what to hold and teach." The Holy Office reader then judged that "there is no need to print this book, or to call attention in any other way to its theses and propositions. Otherwise the book could seem a tacit judgment and condemnation of other and probable theses and criticisms of St. Thomas that are accepted and properly approved in schools and academies. Those ideas should not be castigated and put in the stocks, as we say." Moreover, the innovation of reducing St. Thomas' doctrine to a handbook is dangerous, and would pose great problems for serious scholars. He noted that "Some people wanted to submit the book to the universities, and let them decide after careful scrutiny whether or not to print it. I don't like that idea. Luther used to send his books to the universities for greater clout, and he dedicated one book to Leo IX with that in mind to cover his own intransigence. St. Thomas' doctrine should not be summarized or truncated, but presented whole and entire. If his teaching contains doctrines that are only probable, or less commonly held, or even not now approved by the Church, then professors should advise their students of this, and indicate what theses to keep, and what to discard."

The Pope's illness and subsequent death in turn prevented resolution of the matter, and the speculative part of the *Ratio studiorum* was not returned to the Society until late 1591. It was unchanged. The Holy Office decree read: "The Eminent Cardinals judge that the book the

Fathers of the Society have submitted is to be returned to them. They trust that Father General and the Fathers of the Society will make diligent efforts in their apostolate of public service so that their lecturers and administrators will everywhere remain united in sound teaching."

Chapter 4.
The 1591 *Ratio Studiorum*

A. Preparation and Distribution of Rules (1589-1591)

After careful study of the province responses, the committee first revised *Ratio studiorum 1586A* to produce *Ratio studiorum 1586B*. Then they began to draft rules for the academic officials, according to *Ratio 1586A's* note that "The corpus must be broken down into individual parts, and specific rules or directives drafted for each." That happened from 1589 throughout 1590. Acquaviva's letter to Tucci of 12 August 1590 mentioned the revised rules for the professor of theology. In a letter of 16 September 1590, also to Tucci, the General noted the rules for the Scripture professor that he received and would submit to the Fathers Assistant received review. The rules for teachers of the lower classes arrived on 1 December, and by 15 January 1591 he had the evident satisfaction that "The last rules have been delivered, and we are glad the whole task is done."

As Tucci and his colleagues prepared rules for the schools, Acquaviva had them examined by three Fathers Assistant, as may be inferred from his 12 August 1590 letter to Tucci: "I send Your Reverence the reports of the three Assistants on the *ordo studiorum*, but to save time, they were not read together. If Your Reverence finds any inconsistencies or difficulties in this, please note and forward them to me, and I will resolve the matter." The Fathers Assistant were sent for review not only rules for officials (of the 1591 *Ratio*), but also *Ratio 1586A* and *Ratio 1586B*. They called the first *Liber Excusus* and the latter *Ratio studiorum practica*. Nevertheless, they did not have at hand the text of the rules that was later produced, but only a preliminary version that Tucci and Azor later revised.

The same size as *Ratio studiorum 1586A*, the new book had a shorter title: *Ratio atque institutio studiorum*. Few copies are extant, for, as noted, Acquaviva ordered all those of earlier editions burned once the definitive text reached the provinces in 1599. The book showed more than one innovation. First and most important was the way the matter was presented. *Ratio 1586A/B* comprised treatises on several disciplines, but *Ratio studiorum 1591* included rules for academic officials. In the former edition, the authors set in one place everything they wanted to explain, propose, or regulate for a specific discipline, say, Scripture. In *Ratio 1591,* regulations for Scripture study were scattered (and had to be searched out) among the rules for provincial, rector, dean, and professor of Scripture. So also for all the disciplines. The absence of a *Delectus opinionum* was another major difference. Under the title *Pars speculativa,* that section, extensively rewritten, was submitted under separate cover and in manuscript form to the provinces in 1592. There were no rules for the professor of Apologetics. The few words about the discipline are found in part among the rules for the professors of scholastic theology and Scripture, as well as among the rules *Ultramontanis propriae.*

Following 332 pages of rules for various officials are Appendices, some with rules for particular countries, some with paradigm lectures in the humanities. What was their origin? After study of the *1586 Ratio,* the provinces noted items in the program that needed to be modified for their regions. Rome entered these in *Ratio 1586B,* but they were later removed and sent out as appendices of *Ratio 1591.* Similarly for the lecture paradigms. The first of the *Six Supplementary Chapters Sent to the Provinces in 1586* asked them "to give paradigms and examples for individual schools of the way to explain precepts and authors for student comprehension." Many provinces complied. The Roman committee took the Upper German, Aragon, Polish, Lyons and Austrian province reports to compose *Paradigms or Teaching Methods for Rhetoric and Humanities Classes. Ratio 1586B* promised paradigms: "exegesis proper for the (rhetoric) classes will be illustrated elsewhere with appropriate paradigms that the instructor should follow closely." That promise, repeated verbatim in the *Ratio 1591* rules for the rhetoric professor, was fulfilled in the Appendices. The rules appeared as separate printed fascicules with their own pagination, but are found in only three of the extant copies. The 1599 *Ratio studiorum* dropped them.

The 1591 *Ratio studiorum* was definitive and mandatory for all collegiate houses of the Society. Nevertheless Acquaviva set a trial period to see what needed improvement, according to the preface: "Experience over a three year period should be reported to Father General, so that once the *Ratio* has been amended where needed by his order, it may at last stand firm."

The long sought *Ratio studiorum* finally arrived. How was it received? As to be expected, there was neither complete consensus nor universal joy. Hoffaeus (who left Rome for his province in 1591) spoke frankly to Acquaviva: "About the *Ratio studiorum,* even though it's not easy for me to criticize my superiors' administrative policies, nevertheless, and I say it only for the common good, I fear that unless Your Reverence provides greater incentives to Ours, the project won't have a happy ending. We are used to old ways very different from the new *Ratio*; we cling to them so closely that I don't think we try to overcome the obstacles we meet. We debate rather than experiment to see what to keep, discard, or ignore. Your Reverence should write a letter for everyone (so I don't seem to be its author), urging our men to solve their problems, and, if they want to debate, to do so about how to solve them. They should not work counter to the *Ratio* unless in due time after long experience they report to Rome a consensus of teachers and advisors. Many men here like the *Ratio*, but others don't, and are unwilling to overcome their difficulties. Enough! It's already too much."

Acquaviva had to use his authority in the Austrian province, ordering the provincial: "Your Reverence should scotch a rumor (supposedly rampant in some places) that the *Ratio is* not to be observed the same way everywhere. Until they desist, rumor mongers are to be confronted openly. I am sure you will do so, and they will realize the rumor is false, especially since the *Ratio* has been received and put into practice in many provinces with no delay and with good results. It is Your Reverence's task to effect the same thing in your province, and to overcome all obstacles, which, in fact, you will find are fewer than you fear."

B. THE SPECULATIVE PART OF THE *RATIO STUDIORUM* PUBLISHED (1592)

The Holy Office returned the Speculative Part of the *Ratio* at the end of 1591. About 20 manuscript copies were made and sent to the provinces by July 1592. Its parts comprised Acquaviva's Introduction, Rules *De delectu opinionum,* a Catalog of obligatory propositions, a *Delectus opinionum* for Scripture and Apologetics professors, and a Catalog of optional propositions. Tucci's detailed scholia were omitted. There were six rules about obligatory Society doctrine as in Acquaviva's 1582 directive, with text and sense somewhat changed, even though the 1586 *Ratio* had eleven. The number of propositions increased in both catalogs: the later (1592) ones had 87 and 67, the earlier (1586) catalogs 78 and 49. The preface to the Catalog of optional propositions that was printed as an appendix explained its unusual position a bit surprisingly: "For good reasons we decided not to print the catalog of optional propositions in the order of propositions given above. However, we want rectors, deans, and lecturers to have it at hand, and to know that they should follow St. Thomas, but if they choose to follow another opinion, that it is in these propositions only that they are free to do so." "Good reasons *(iustae causae)"* was the term of the Holy Office reader's report. Also, for the same "good reasons" the Speculative Part of the *Ratio studiorum* was not printed. Acquaviva promulgated the *Pars practica* of the *1591 Ratio* with an order for three years intense experimentation. In contrast, the *Pars speculativa* got none, but had immediate definitive obligatory force, as the General's preface insisted: "We commend this formula, carefully drafted by many teachers, with all our power and authority, to all of Ours in literary (higher) studies."

C. THE *RATIO STUDIORUM* AND THE FIFTH GENERAL CONGREGATION (1593-1594)

1. *PARS SPECULATIVA*

While *Ratio studiorum 1591* was being tested in the Society's schools in 1592-1593, Rome and the provinces prepared for an extraordinary general congregation that would play a large part in *Ratio* history. Pope Clement VIII ordered a congregation at the behest of troublemakers who wanted a new order of things in Spain. The *Acta* of the preparatory province congregations frequently mentioned the program of studies. Often found there was the substance of a Roman province petition: "that a *Liber Studiorum* treating both *Delectus opinionum* and practice be officially recognized, and stability here assured." Accordingly, the general congregation (convoked on 21 December 1592, convened on 3 November 1593) set one of its twelve committees with Robert Bellarmine, then Roman College rector, as chairman, to consider approbation of the *Ratio studiorum*. Also appointed were I. Tyrius, a Scot and German Assistant, B. Castori, provincial of Lyons, L. Richeome, provincial of Aquataine, B. Rossignoli, provincial of Milan, I. Chastellier, provincial of France, M. M. Marcos, I. Correa, B. Oliver, and A. Saphor.

As they started work, the members were warned by a special committee "De detrimentis" that "Freedom to teach and endorse the many scandalous opinions temerarious in faith and practice, has no place now. Unless Jesuits are somehow effectively restrained, we fear they will be denounced to the Tribunal of the Inquisition (which has happened more than once), or that even greater evils will come." That pessimism Father Ribadeneyra passed on to the Congregation: "The times are dangerous. Some Jesuits engage in unbridled speculation, and we have many enemies. The Congregation must weigh whether it should delimit with rigorous new decrees matters treated broadly in the *Constitutions,* and to order Ours, in Spain at least, to hold by their teeth Blessed Thomas' every doctrine, save one or two, and to order that anyone doing otherwise by teaching new opinions diverging from common doctrine be severely punished." He suggested Father General designate two or three priests in each province to review doctrines. That would restrain Jesuits, and lift a heavy burden from Superiors, who were often embarrassed by their teachings.

The committee, "after some days of intense meetings and discussion," brought the Congregation its report, the *Relatio deputatorum pro studiis,* with recommendations about the *Pars speculativa* and the *Delectus opinionum.* They had seven principles for teaching, five rules for theologians for choice of opinions, and five for philosophers. The General Congregation accepted the recommendations. First, it voted unanimously that Jesuit professors should follow St. Thomas' teaching in scholastic theology as solid, certain, approved, and consistent with the *Constitutions.* Next, the rules drafted by the committee for choice of opinions in philosophy and theology should be entered into the text of the *Ratio studiorum,* and "our professors should observe them carefully." Also approved were its preparatory notes for "better understanding of the Rules." They decreed too that all this, carefully written and revised by the committee, was to be entered into the *Acta Congregationis,* not for everyone's eyes, but "for the use of Superiors for greater elucidation, as well as for learning the Congregation's mind in enacting these rules, and for implementing them."

The text was revised, corrected, and improved by the Congregation, and recorded in the *Acta Congregationis* as the preface to the rules *De delectu opinionum.* It had four paragraphs; the second and third became the second and third rules for the professor of scholastic theology in the 1599 *Ratio studiorum;* the fourth showed as the ninth rule for the provincial. Canon 9 of the Congregation expressed concisely the immense change the *Pars speculativa* admitted: "Jesuit professors of scholastic theology should follow the teaching of St. Thomas according to the practice decreed in the text of the *Ratio studiorum* and explained by Father General. They are not to be appointed to chairs of theology unless they show themselves favorable to the teaching of St. Thomas, and those who are not shall be deprived of their teaching posts." And so, after years of countless meetings, debates, decrees, and immense lists of mandatory and optional theses with long and short scholia, the few lines of canon 9 of the Fifth General Congregation legislated doctrine in philosophy and theology that the Society was to profess. The canon, some rules, and directions for their use, did it all.

Provincial postulates about the *Pars speculativa* were answered in those terms. To the Roman province, Acquaviva wrote that "what pertains to the *Pars speculativa de delectu opinionum* appears in canon 9 with an accompanying explanation." He replied in the same way to Poland, Upper Germany, Belgium, and Naples. (The explanation was the Congregation's decree 56.) In 1594, Father Ximenes, Secretary of the Society, sent the provincials excerpts from the *Acta* that dealt with Society teaching, including the preface to the *Regulae de delectu opinionum* and the *Regulae* themselves. Even so, the Congregation's resolute and solemn actions did not radically solve the multiplex problems about uniformity and orthodoxy of Society teaching. Soon after, Acquaviva himself had to intervene to eradicate some deviations.

2. *PRAXIS ET ORDO STUDIORUM*

When the Fifth General Congregation convened on 3 November 1593, the Society's schools had been experimenting with *Praxis et Ordo Studiorum* for two years. The 1591 *Ratio studiorum,* as noted, was not found entirely satisfactory everywhere. The schools had many problems implementing the new plan. For example, the Neapolitan congregation's *Acta* recorded that "since we have already met many difficulties in the *Ratio studiorum* the General sent us, and are daily finding more that are not easily resolved, we ask the General Congregation to delegate some members to collect these problems for study." The Toledo province asked three theology professors (Blase Rengifo, Francisco Suárez, and Gabriel Vasquez) to analyze the prescriptions in *Praxis et Ordo Studiorum.* According to their report, "its higher study rules (were) not right for the Society, and surely not for the Spanish provinces, because of the immense number that touch even the smallest details. It is impossible to get a general rule for all countries and provinces, given the diverse customs, structures, practices, needs, and other factors it ought to accommodate."

The Belgian province congregation reported the same difficulty: "Although the law, precepts, and directives of the *Ratio studiorum* were firmly approved, as the *Acta* record, and will, we hope, be very useful, still, many items can hardly be implemented in the two Belgian universities due to their laws and customs and our own private reasons. May it please Your Paternity to hear in a fatherly way what Father Provincial and his delegates propose." The Polish congregation asked that "some learned and scholarly members of the Congregation of diverse nationalities, and other than those who drafted the *Ratio studiorum,* be delegated for its total revision, and as far as possible, let every province and country have its say. And make the text brief."

The Congregation was concerned about the problems and projects of the educational apostolate. After the General heard its comments and proposals, he ordered the provincials "to share their difficulties with each other," so that "final decisions can be made about how to accommodate each one." From this came documents with the desiderata and proposals from the various regions, as well as the General's replies. A letter of Father Domenichi, Secretary of the Society, dated 21 December 1595, to Father Charles Reggio, Roman province provincial, advised him of Acquaviva's concessions in the matter of studies.

Spain too, after the General Congregation, conferred about the study program. A report, written at the time, gives a succinct account: "Father Garcías Alarcón, Visitor of the Castilian and Toledan provinces, asked six expert and learned members to study the text of the *Ratio studiorum,* the report the Spanish fathers gave to Rome, and Father General's response. They were to discuss these documents among themselves, and record their conclusions." They replied: "1. Generally speaking, it seems neither possible nor advantageous for the entire Society to be of one mind, or to be made to agree about the many particular items contained in these rules. Given the spread of places and resources and the vibrant diversity of provincial customs and educational structures, our ideas about what faculties to develop and our plans for them also show a great diversity. 2. In many respects it will be necessary to separate Spaniards from other groups, and even in Spain itself, we shall have to distinguish one province from another, and in a single province one collegiate house from another, insofar as they are associated with the local universities, and must meet their standards and requirements, if Jesuit studies and literary exercises are to merit a splendid reputation and enjoy external accreditation."

Given what Father Acquaviva conceded to various regions for implementation of the *Ratio studiorum* (after his unsuccessful attempt to get maximum possible uniformity in the Society), we can see that here after much deliberation the Society at last returned to St. Ignatius' principle in the *Constitutions:* "As for specified lecture hours, their order and method, and exercises both written and oral in the various faculties, public addresses, and discourses, all this will be treated elsewhere in a document approved by the General." The *Constitutions* then urge that "it be adapted to the places, times, and persons involved, even though they should follow its norms as much as can be." Acquaviva's response to the Upper German province accorded quite well with that advice: "Provincials should consult with each other about practical matters of implementation to learn what is best for each province. Nevertheless, you do have the duty of adhering as closely as possible to the prescribed *Ratio studiorum.*"

CHAPTER 5.
THE 1599 *RATIO STUDIORUM*

The Fifth General Congregation finished work on the Speculative Part of the *Ratio studiorum,* but much more had to be done on the rules for studies. In 1595 the Secretary of the Society wrote that he was unable to send the provinces Father General's concessions in the matter of lower studies because "so much has occurred that we are unable to classify and send promptly what we have recorded." Acquaviva mentioned a new development in a response (quoted in part above) to the Roman provincial congregation: "Decisions about choice of opinions that pertain to the Speculative Part have been made, and can be found in Canon 9; an instruction has been forwarded. Matters touching practice have been referred to some Jesuits of Italy."

Who were the Jesuits newly put to the task after the general congregation? Not Tucci, who by then gravely ill died in January 1597. Father Brunelli, who helped him for many years with the *litterae humaniores* parts, was surely one. The Gregorian University library in Rome has a copy of the 1591 *Ratio studiorum* worn thin by his fingers and copiously annotated in preparation for revision of the rules. Philip Rinaldi, who met endless objections to endlessly revised rules, was another. A third was Horace Torsellini, a rector in the provinces from 1591 to 1595, and brought to Rome in 1596 where he held the offices of confessor and prefect of elocution until his death in 1599. Brunelli's notes show that he worked with both: on 17 December 1598, for instance, he quoted Torsellini to Rinaldi three times about a debate over a particular point in the order of studies.

Revision work took three years (1595-1598) to produce a series of rules: first, the incomplete Brunelli text with rules only for professors of lower classes (rhetoric, humanities, first, second, and third grammar levels). The content of the rules Brunelli listed completely in the right margin of the pages. The left margins showed numerous annotations: "superfluous," "get a common rule," "put elsewhere," "shorten," "too trivial," " go easier," etc. Other texts came later; we can identify chronologically four families, designated by capital letters: the texts *Ratio studiorum 91/A B C D.* Text 91A is almost that of the 1591 *Ratio,* but text 91D almost completely that of the 1599 *Ratio.*

Rule revision lasted until 1598, as we learn from a Rinaldi report: "Final Revision and Emendation of the *Ratio studiorum,* Tusculum. May 1598." Its first part is "Items in the revision of the *Ratio* for review or proposal to Father General," then "Items revised by the committee at Tusculum, May 1598," and, in a separate folio, "Father General's decisions after the book was reviewed in his presence." The revision committee tried, as far as possible, to make a table of the notes and requests of the provinces. There was unanimous petition to shorten the list of rules: many of the same rules appear in several places; the rules for piety and devotion, for example, were duplicated in the rules of all the teachers. Probably the idea was that each one have a complete set of rules for his office, but not the entire book. To avoid this duplication, common rules were adopted for all professors in the higher faculties, and also for teachers in the lower ones. For greater brevity some rules were dropped, and others put more concisely. There were far fewer rules. The 1591 *Ratio* had 837, the 1599 *Ratio* 467; the provincial first had 96 rules, then only 40.

Another goal was to avoid unduly great uniformity in applying the *Ratio.* Acquaviva, as noted, granted many concessions to that end after the Fifth General Congregation. The concern can be detected at work in their editing of the rules, where most of all in D text, but also in C, many qualifiers were introduced: "if the situation allows," "modify according to local usage," "where needed," "at the instructor's discretion." This way, prescriptive rules were mitigated.

The text had no *Pars speculativa* or *Delectus opinionum;* the Fifth General Congregation sent its decisions about them in manuscript form to the provinces. In the printed text they were prudentially omitted, save that the rules for the professors of Scripture and scholastic theology gave principles about the doctrine they were to profess. The *Appendices* of the 1591 *Ratio* were also dropped. Father General later gave special concessions in implementing the *Ratio* to the provincials in individually addressed notes, perhaps to make their temporary character and the consequent possibility of changing and adapting them to new needs more evident. A completely new series of rules was attached: seminar (*academiae*) rules, and the rules for repeating higher studies, for example.

The book's 1599 Neapolitan edition was the principal one. Others came shortly later: at Mainz in 1600, again at Naples in 1603, and at Rome in

1608, 1610, and 1616. The Seventh General Congregation revised and approved the text in 1616, leaving it unchanged apart from modifications in the rules for provincials about the studies of Jesuit scholastics.

All this left the Society with an unanticipated rigidity. But did later generations forget the Ignatian principle in the *Constitutions,* defined by the Fifth General Congregation, and handed on to posterity, that the *Ratio* must be adapted to the times according to new needs of place and people? If, in fact, the *Ratio* text stayed fixed, in practice nevertheless, many, often profound, innovations were made, especially in the eighteenth century. In Austria, for example, in 1773 (the year the Society was suppressed), Jesuits were teaching German in 7 colleges, French in 12, Italian in 3, Bohemian in 2, Hungarian in 6, German literature in 2, history in 5, geography in one, architecture in 3, geometry in 3, technical drawing in 2, mechanics in 5, hydrography in one (Trieste), agronomy in one, and economics in 2.

MATHEMATICS IN THE JESUIT *RATIO STUDIORUM*

Giuseppe Cosentino

The origin of the model that even today molds European scholastic curricula, save technical and professional ones, from elementary school up to university, is the *Ratio studiorum* promulgated by Claude Acquaviva, fifth General Superior (1580-1615) of the Society of Jesus. The *Ratio studiorum* merits this historic importance, for it was not just a theoretical plan, but a schema that animated the organization and foundation of the first unified secondary education system Europe ever knew. Arguably, creation of the system was a key event that, along with the rise of new economic and social structures, and a new understanding of science, helped bring about the modern world.

Educational theorists and cultural historians have identified Humanism and Classicism in the *Ratio studiorum*, the pedagogical methods it adopted, and other such features. Science historians, however, have not studied the *Ratio*, despite the importance of many Jesuit scientists, and mathematics teachers in the Society's schools especially, for seventeenth- and eighteenth-century science history. Also, many first rank figures attended Jesuit schools; among the scientists, take Descartes, educated at the College of La Flèche.

In fact, up to the last quarter of the eighteenth century, many of the better youth of continental Europe, including Poland and Hungary, did pre-university studies at Jesuit schools. (The British Isles had schools too, and many English lads came to study in continental Jesuit colleges.) It is then important for the history of modern science to ascertain in Jesuit education the presence and weight accorded in the Society's teaching to "scientific" (in the late 1500s sense) topics that were specifically "mathematics." So, using Jesuit documents primarily, we shall try to reconstruct the vicissitudes of the material from its first appearance at a Jesuit college (in Messina) up to promulgation of the definitive text of the official 1599 *Ratio studiorum*. More than just explicating the 1599 *Ratio's* few, spare remarks about mathematics; we must study them as the end product of the entire formation and consolidation process over the development history of the Society's *Ratio studiorum* itself.

1. FROM JEROME NADAL'S FIRST MATHEMATICS PROGRAM (1548) TO THE *CONSTITUTIONS* (1553/4)

Ignatius wrote the *Constitutions* between 1541 and 1550, adding new parts and revising others up to his death in 1556. This fundamental text defined the life of the Society of Jesus. The Fourth Part on studies *(De iis qui in Societate retinentur instruendis in litteris et aliis quae ad proximos adjuvandos conferunt)* has two sections: its first ten chapters (Ignatius wrote most in 1550) regulate the colleges. Chapters 11-17, dating to the end of 1553 or early 1554, treat Jesuit-sponsored universities.[1]

Chapters 12-15 comprise ordinances for the higher study courses.[2] Ignatius intended that "commonly in the colleges *Litterae Humaniores*, languages, and Christian Doctrine, and, if necessary, some reading of Cases of Conscience, be presented. If anyone can preach appropriately, or hear confessions, that should be done too. But there is to be no treatment of the higher sciences. Rather those in the colleges who have excelled in *Litterae Humaniores* should be sent to the Society's universities to learn these sciences."[3] His directive, however, was not always honored. The larger colleges often had philosophy and theology courses, to the chagrin of St. Ignatius' secretary, Juan de Polanco.[4]

The First General Congregation approved the *Constitutions* with few modifications in 1558, two years after the death of the Order's founder, and this left the text of Ignatius almost unchanged.

The *Constitutions* limit themselves to giving general criteria, letting for the most part a future directive fix particulars for the order of lectures and exercises, curriculum content, and details about teaching: "prescribed hours for lectures, their order and manner, composition exercises (which the instructor should correct), disputations in the various faculties, public speeches and poetry will be treated in detail in a document approved by Father General, to which this constitution refers us, while urging that all be accommodated to places, times, and persons, even though its directives should be observed as far as possible."[5]

Invaluable experience was had after Ignatius wrote these chapters, and from this came directives, programs, and didactic methods that won a first, mostly positive, review. Here we note especially the experience of the College of Messina which began higher courses in 1548. Jerome Nadal's scholastic programs grew, or were basically formulated from that experience. In August 1553, at the request of Martin de Olave, Roman College director and professor of theology, Nadal composed for the Roman College (founded in 1551, though higher courses only began in

1553), the *Order of Lectures and Exercises in Universities of the Society of Jesus.*

The College of Messina was the first in Italy to instruct extern students. Beginning after Easter of 1548, courses in logic, scholastic theology, Greek and Hebrew were developed in the higher faculty.[6] At the end of September, in view of the opening of the first regular scholastic year, the rector, Jerome Nadal,[7] compiled and sent to Rome for approval the *Laws ... and Constitutions*[8] of the College. These also included a brief and specific mathematics program. It stood apart from those of the other higher courses, such as philosophy (logic), scholastic theology, Greek and Hebrew, insofar as it specified study texts and their order of explication, while the directives for the rest were of an organizational and didactic nature only: "[The mathematics professor] will read mathematics outside the regular order at a time the Rector shall deem best: first, some books of Euclid, until the students are familiar with the demonstrations, then the *Practical Arithmetic* of Orontius, and his *Sphere,* Stobler's *Astrolabe,* and Peurbach's *Theoricae.*"[9]

Here was an ambitious program that put mathematics on a par with the other disciplines. In addition to Euclid's *Elements,* the texts were among the best then available: the *Practical Arithmetic in Four Books,* and the *World Sphere,* or *Cosmography,* of Orontius Finaeus, the *Construction and Use of the Astrolabe* by John Stoeffler, and George Peurbach's *New Planetary Theory.*[10] Together they comprised in current editions about 1300-1400 pages, not counting Euclid's *Elements.* The time and intellectual maturity which students working from elementary geometry and arithmetic needed to understand the complicated schemes of planetary motion according to Ptolemaic theory ("until they are familiar with the demonstrations"), was clearly not something that should be demanded for topics of only minor importance.

Nadal was a very cultured man. Besides knowing Scripture, Greek, Hebrew, Scholastic and Dogmatic Theology, he was a good mathematician who had taught the science at Paris: "Nadal is learned in mathematics, which he read in Paris (as I believe you know), and quite diligent at it."[11] According to Polanco, Nadal also taught the mathematics program at Messina from the start of the scholastic year 1549/50.[12]

We learn from a Nadal letter that there were two mathematics courses, one "in public school."[13] A second Nadal document, in 1552, strengthened and adjusted the mathematics program of the 1548 directives. His *De studii generalis dispositione et ordine* outlined a three-year mathematics course for the first and third years of which the 1548 program provided the material: "The first reading is from Euclid and from a practical arithmetic, as well as from astronomical principles, the so-called *Sphere.* Unless something more useful appears, this should be the *Cosmographia* of Orontius. The first reading will treat these principles, and occupy the first year; it will also be offered yearly. Let as much Euclid as possible be read, since practical arithmetic and the *Sphere* do not usually need that much time. It is appropriate in this reading to explain some topics from other branches of mathematics, for example, from Regiomontanus' *De omnimodis triangulis* or from Jordanus, etc."[14] The program began with geometry and arithmetic and continued with cosmography. To defer astronomy to third year allowed an in-depth study of Euclid, as well as introduction to the trigonometry needed for a better idea of the motions and relative positions of the celestial bodies. The specified texts, apart from Orontius Finaeus, were the *De triangulis* of Johannes Mueller and the *De triangulis* of Jordanus Nemorarius.[15] The third year had an extended treatment of astronomy. "The third lecture each year will treat astronomy, starting with *Theoria planetarum.* Topics can always be taken from Ptolemy's *Great Synthesis (Almagest),* or at least from the *Epitome* of Regiomontanus, the *Alphonsine Tables,* the *Astrolabe,* etc."[16]

To expand the earlier program into two years was a notable accomplishment: The *Astrolabe* and the *Theory of Planets* stayed, and the *Alphonsine Tables* were there, but, above all, the Ptolemaic text could be brought into the lectures, or at least something from Mueller's *Epitome of Ptolemy's Almagest.*[17] As Reinhold, commenting on Peurbach, noted in his preface to *Theoricae novae,* the difference between that work and those of Ptolemy and Regiomontanus was not so much their goals as their depth of treatment: "There are two kinds of explanation. One gives only the *to hoti* (το οτι) of the art: bare and brief principles, either propositions or rules, are givens, but without reason or demonstration. The second kind gives also the *dioti,* (διοτι), that is, bare propositions and rules are not just repeated, but proper causes are carefully analyzed, effects and demonstrations are unified. That is how the *Almagest* and Regiomontanus's *Epitome* give the *dioti* of astronomical motion and phenomena. But this *Isagoge* has almost the *to hoti* only of the art: it has a simple statement of the Sun's motion but no explanation or reasons for it."[18]

Optics and the theory of music came in second year, which had all the program's physics [natural philosophy]. "The second lecture treats music theory and perspective. Either the common text, or Witelo's, is read for perspective, for music, either Fabius Stapula's text, or some more convenient one. Some practical geometry and mensuration, taken from any author, may be put in this lecture, etc." Witelo's treatise *De natura, ratione, et projectione radiorum visus, luminum, colorum, atque formarum, quam vulgo Perspectivum vocant, libri X,*[19] was recommended for perspective; for music theory, the *Musica libris quattuor demonstrata*[20] of Fabius Stapula (Lefevre d'Etaples).

Nadal's second document had a nature and purpose very different from the first, which gave the rules of the College of Messina and the courses and programs that were actually taught. But here, as Lukacs rightly noted (in his new edition of this and other first period Society education papers), we have a preparatory text for the *De studiis* chapters in the Ignatian *Constitutions*. In March 1552 Ignatius asked Nadal to read and annotate parts of the *Constitutions*. The annotations were due in Rome that year by the end of October. His document can be taken at least as a partial response to Ignatius.

Nadal treated at length higher studies: languages (Greek, Hebrew, and Oriental), the arts course (philosophy and mathematics), and theology. Mathematics he set complementary to the natural philosophy and metaphysics course. Because the latter was afforded treatment equal to that for mathematics, it became a three year course, and the entire arts course four years, with the first one for logic: "In the last three years, or so, those entering the program will profess natural philosophy and metaphysics, that is, Aristotle's *De physico auditu (8 books), De caelo (4), De meteorologicis (4), De generatione et corruptione (2), De anima (3), Parva Naturalia* and *Metaphysica (12)*. Three readers are to read them in three classes, at least by the program's third year." The philosophers had four hours of class: two for lectures, two for repetition of the lectures. "This gives them time to hear the mathematics lecture."[21]

Every day, however, the professor was to have a single mathematics lecture for each of the three classes of "metaphysics" (=physics or metaphysics, to distinguish these students from those in the first year arts logic course). "The mathematics professor will also read lectures, and he will have no other daily assignment, except that he himself will repeat the lecture heard with the preceptor present; he assigns his own thesis defenders for monthly and annual disputations. He will arrange his prelections so as to read one lecture the first year there are students in logic and physics (only the physics students are to hear mathematics); two lectures the second year, three the third, and always three after that."[22] This way, one reader would do for a three-year mathematics course.

Promotion of the Gandía (Spain) and Messina public schools to university status moved Ignatius to seek appropriate guidelines and a specific paradigm for the Society to use in all future efforts, as well as general criteria for the *Constitutions*. Messina proved useful for such a paradigm. Ignatius valued Nadal's 1548 plan of studies so much that he approved it with few changes. In December 1550 Claude Le Jay wrote to Ignatius from Germany: "What authors should we read for grammar, rhetoric, philosophy, and theology? Please answer with the list the Messina college published of its readers and lectures."[23] For some time Messina was the only paradigm; its schools were the first examples of the *modus parisiensis* adapted to the orientation and needs of the Society of Jesus.[24] The Roman College, founded in 1551, had schools of grammar and humanities; students of the German College, established the next year, also came there to finish their studies in philosophy and theology. For that reason Ignatius entrusted to Father Martino de Olave, both the Roman College rectorship and the task of preparing a studies document for the Society's university. Olave probably delivered it complete in the summer of 1553.[25]

Olave's *Ordo lectionum et exercitationum in universitatibus Societatis Iesu* shortened the philosophy course in Nadal's program from four to three years.[26] Olave, a theologian, did not try to give specific directives for the mathematics course, but simply recommended adequate treatment. "Besides the Aristotelian professors there should also be someone to read mathematics as well as the good and useful parts of astrology. This will be at an hour that lets the Aristotle scholars as a group hear and compare that art with Aristotle's doctrine."[27] The horarium prescribed an hour of lecture each day except in the first semester. This made the mathematics course two-and-a-half-years.[28]

Right away, however, mathematics got a lesser role in Roman College practice, which it later kept in Jesuit schools. In the scholastic year 1553/54 the instructor, Balthasar Torres, also read natural philosophy, counter to Olave's idea of assigning mathematics instruction to an appointed reader. Harsh reality probably was decisive right away in curtailing the program, and, even more, in limiting foundation of chairs of mathematics. To find Jesuit professors able to teach the highly technical courses Nadal prescribed was not easy. Natural philosophy teachers like Torres were surely competent to teach brief and summary complementary mathematics courses, but specialists were needed for an expanded three-year program. At times they were recruited from outside the Society, for example, Maurolyco, who taught at Messina.[29] But this was always exceptional, and could not solve the problem. Clavius, as we shall see, deplored this dearth of academic specialists. For him, the task of teacher formation was basic to the struggle to assure the Society and the Church the scientists he believed were of vital importance. Ignatius doubtless thought the role of mathematics in Nadal's program, and even in Olave's, was excessive.

Nadal, at one time mathematics professor in Paris, surely knew the conflict between the university and French humanists that centered on language and mathematics. In 1531 Francis I founded six Royal Chairs in the university, thanks above all to the efforts of the Humanist Budé. Languages were given five: three for Hebrew, two for Greek. Mathematics had one,[30] entrusted specifically to Orontius Finaeus, whose texts were central in Nadal's program. Later, a chair for physical science, astronomy, geography, and medicine was also created.

Ignatius welcomed Greek, Hebrew, and even oriental languages (that missionaries needed) into the Society's *ratio studiorum* and codified them in the *Constitutions*.[31] But strong mathematics programs were not necessarily assured a presence on account of the proper needs of the Order and its schools, the objective of which was, and remained, the formation of theologians and missionaries.

The *Constitutions* refer briefly to mathematics, but only to fix some criteria as normative, indicating explicitly the Roman College policy of making mathematics complementary to physics as a specific paradigm for items that had no place in the *Constitutions*. "Accommodate Roman College rules to other cases as befits each."[32]

The sole concession to mathematics teaching occurs in a "Declaration," where Ignatius confirmed subordination of "profane sciences" to the Society's apostolic goal: "Logic, metaphysics, moral science, and mathematics to the extent that it accords with the goal proposed for us are to be taught."[32bis] What was "the goal proposed for us" found clear explanation in the Preface: "Since the goal to which the Society rightly tends is to help attain the ultimate end of one's own soul and that of the neighbor's, for which they were created, and since for this, in addition to the example of one's life, both learning and a way of explaining it are necessary . . . in those admitted to probation, . . . we must treat Letters and the way to use this knowledge."[33] This is no sterile affirmation of principle, intended to stand without consequence, but rather a point of permanent reference, operative in the Ignatian vision. The goal was already clear in the Fifth Chapter material about the studies of Jesuit scholastics: "The goal of learning in the Society is to help, with God's grace, one's own soul and our neighbor's. This is the norm, in general and for particular persons. What disciplines Ours should learn, and how far they should progress in them should be decided accordingly. Generally speaking, the literature of various languages, logic, natural and moral philosophy, metaphysics and theology, both scholastic and positive, and Sacred Scripture help to this end. Those sent to the colleges should do studies in these disciplines, and some will work with greater effort in those that the prefect of studies shall judge more fitting in the Lord, taking into account time, place, and persons, etc."[34]

This idea became more precise in the chapter on studies in the Society's universities: "Since the goal of the Society and of studies is to help our neighbor to a knowledge and love of God and the salvation of his soul, and since the faculty of theology is a more apt means to this end, the Society's universities should make special efforts in this regard."[34bis] What distinguished this chapter (of 1553/4) from the earlier one (written at the start of 1550), apart from their diverse objects, was the intentional ranking of disciplines in a list showing a hierarchy of functionally interrelated sciences relative to theology, which represented the "knowledge and love of God," and so set the goal for the rest. In chapter five, theology ended a seemingly casual order. Here it tops a ladder with carefully indicated steps: "Because the teaching of theology as well as its use demands, especially today, knowledge of humane letters, and Latin, Greek, and Hebrew too, suitable professors, in good number, should be prepared for this purpose. Instructors can be readied for other practical languages, Chaldee, Arabic, and Hindi, when these seem needed or useful for the goal proposed, remembering the different regions' needs and the reasons for teaching them." Moreover, philosophy and other sciences should be studied insofar as they prepare the mind for the study of theology. Through theology these disciplines aim at the salvation of souls: "So also since the arts and natural sciences dispose the mind to theology and aid its perfect knowledge and use, and by themselves help to that goal, they should be taught with equal care, and by competent instructors, sincerely seeking in all things God's honor and glory."[34ter]

Ignatius recommended following Aristotle closely in the philosophical and natural disciplines: "In logic, natural and moral philosophy, and metaphysics, Aristotle's doctrine should be followed."[35]

What mathematics then included (which, after arithmetic, geometry, and later, algebra, was in part mechanics, perspective or optics, music theory, astronomy, cosmography, geography, astrology, and surveying) had nothing directly relevant to the goal proposed for Jesuit teaching, in contrast to philosophy, and specifically to those "arts or natural sciences" which "disposed the mind to theology" insofar as they were a rational organization of all human experience of the world.

Existence of a basic rapport between the various disciplines and theology as the criterion for admitting them into the studies curriculum, and for their value after admission, was already affirmed by St. Ignatius in the August 1553 *Ratio ordinandi studii universitatis Campostellanae* where "the parts of mathematics a theologian should know" were in fact listed among the topics for study.[36] Yet this doctrinal and purely internal logic could not be pushed to the limit, if for no other reason than that the Society was always realistic about its agenda that necessarily took it into a fast changing external world. Born as a militant organization to struggle in the world, the Society never saw theology as an end in itself, but only as a proper means for the salvation of souls.[37]

Jesuit action never showed abstract doctrinal rigidity, but rather an ability to adapt means to ends. Great pragmatism, with adamance about nonnegotiable goals and principles, marked the Society early on in its academic work also. In 1548, Ignatius' secretary, Juan de Polanco, saw literary, philosophical, and theological formation as means to the Society's goal, and urged that formation look to the more important areas, for example, heresy and heretics. "To see more necessary matters as more important, or to treat carefully critical topics, is a rational policy, e.g., topics that relate to heretics, and those more useful for preaching, hearing confessions, etc."[38] Cosmography too had a place among the sciences for study.[39]

For the rest, the *Constitutions'* directives allowed adaptation for all the various special cases,[40] nor did they preclude future changes new times might demand. Ignatius left his successors to compose a coherent rule and specific regulations for studies in the Society, but urged that all be adapted to places, times, and persons ("advising however that they be accommodated to places, times, and persons, although they should accord with that document, as far as possible." See above.)

Mathematical sciences continued to gain importance in the latter half of the sixteenth century, and forced into question ever more openly the Aristotelian system of sciences. Although at first the two developed at the same time, the day was near when the position Osiander quietly attributed to Copernicus (heliocentrism is only a mathematical hypothesis) would become the Old World system's last defense. (See, for example, Bellarmine's remarks, which also gave the official Church position, on the admissibility of heliocentrism as a purely mathematical hypothesis, so as to better "save the appearances" for planetary motions.)[40bis]

The forty years between the appearance of *De revolutionibus orbium coelestium* (1543) and the Church's condemnation of Copernicanism (February 1616) saw the mathematical sciences change from purely practical procedures in astronomy, astrology, business, navigation, computation of time, surveying, and so on, to a world-view at variance with the traditional one fixed in the Aristotelian encyclopedia of science. Ignatius could hardly anticipate all that when he wrote the *Constitutions,* but his reasons were important and had considerable weight in the formation of the Society's *Ratio studiorum* in the second half of the century (1547-1599), the era of "pacific" development of the new sciences. "Jesuit professors were at that time challenged by the difficult but vital task of stopping secularization of literature and science."[41]

We shall see that in the last quarter of the sixteenth century Christopher Clavius, the most renowned Jesuit scientist of his day, sought in Plato grounds for the cognitive and not merely practical value of mathematics. Clavius tried to get for it the respect accorded philosophy in the ordinances for studies. Though not completely successful, his work had real value in assuring high level Society presence in research and scientific debate for several decades

2. THE SPREAD OF JESUIT COLLEGES AND UNIVERSITIES.
THE *MODUS ROMANUS*

The Society's founder wanted the Roman schools to serve as models for the many Jesuit colleges that would be associated with them even before the *Ratio studiorum* was promulgated. Ignatius wanted the Society's experience to mature into a complete and definitive plan of studies. To be sure, he realized how innovative its task was. His many references to the *modus parisiensis* are not a call for its passive adoption and use, but rather for development of a quite original *modus romanus,* even if inspired by goals and standards up to then identified with the University of Paris.

Implementation, in theory worldwide, of a post-elementary school to university faculty instructional system was the grandiose, unprecedented plan that took shape between 1548 and the foundation of the Roman College that was to be its paradigm and operative center. "The College's plan and purpose will be general" for three reasons: first, because "it is advisable to test the form for like colleges and *studia generalia* in the Society's keeping"; second, "(because) many Jesuits from various lands have not completed their studies, . . . it will be very convenient to form a *collegium generale* where briefly Ours, giving time to Letters, work entirely to develop their ability both to teach those well disposed to receive the truth, and also to win over those resistant and inimical to it." Last, "it helps to have a seminary especially for northern nations (alluding to the German College, founded in 1552, as noted) where the Catholic religion suffers so much, in which men of those nations are taught with example and sound doctrine by persons of their own language to keep what remains, and restore what was lost, of the Christian religion."[42] This way the Roman College was not only a paradigm for all Society schools, but also a "forge" for teachers and "operarii" from all Europe missioned to various works everywhere. The ratio between religious and extern students was very high. Later, institutions like the German College were added for other nationalities, as well as the Roman Seminary in 1564. Because all their seminarians studied in the Roman College, it became in large part an internal service for both the Society and the Church in the formation of Jesuit instructors and secular clergy.[43] And so the *Ratio Studiorum* would evolve most of all in the Roman College, with elaboration of structures, study plans, and documents.

A 1566 manuscript[44] gave a specific plan of studies for the College. The directive about classes in the Arts Faculty is almost the same as the definitive one.[45] Mathematics figures as a supplementary topic in the second year. "The mathematics professor lectures in this order: Six books of Euclid, arithmetic, the *Sphere*, cosmography, astrology, planetary theory, Alphonsine tables, with perspective for sundials. Only second-year philosophers attend these lectures, and occasionally, logicians, with permission." This program seems to follow closely Nadal's program of 1552, even to identical ordering of disciplines. However, it is a one, not a three-year program, and this makes a big difference how the matter is taught. Silence about authors and texts suggests that compendia, themselves little more than introductions to the disciplines, had come into use. In fact, the program is, in part, found elsewhere at the time. For example, in the University of Salamanca the mathematics professor explained "[in] the second year six books of Euclid, arithmetic to square and cube roots, Ptolemy's *Almagest,* or Regiomontanus' *Epitome,* or Geber, or Copernicus, at the auditors' pleasure as a substitute, the *Sphere*."

Third year has cosmography and geography.[46] This is a two-year course, between what Nadal wanted and what the Roman College had. Disciplines and sequence are the same, and the texts selected among the better ones (Copernicus stands out right away!), though with fewer options than Nadal's program. So we may infer that a standard mathematics program was then in place, and taught on a more or less advanced level with direct reading of original texts or use of simple manuals, as time allowed.

An articulated, fully detailed *Ratio studiorum* had to meet three requirements: it had to be internally coherent, compatible with the Society's goals and cultural orientation, and relevant to the external scene, insofar as the Society was becoming the largest Christian body given to educating youth.

Ledesma's treatise,[47] dated to early 1575, the year he died, did not aim to be a mere directive to fix job descriptions for professors and officials, class sequences, course material, study programs, or lecture hours. Rather, it looked to give a logically tight symbiosis for the disciplines involved. Its synoptic table uniquely witnesses to a highly unified synthesis with authoritative precedent in one carefully taken from the *Constitutions*, Part 4, chapter 12, which required all studies to be directed to the Society's ultimate goal. Ledesma made the table to show the interdependence of the subjects he would treat systematically in *De ratione et ordine studiorum Collegii Romani*,[48] though he did not get beyond discussion of the humanities class. His synoptic table put the mathematical disciplines among the liberal arts, along with moral philosophy and the arts course that comprised logic, physics, and metaphysics. In its complexity the schema resembled that of the *Consuetudines* and corresponded to the definitive schema fixed in the *Ratio et institutio studiorum*.

Fortunately, Ledesma left a brief manuscript, *De artium liberalium studiis*,[49] a draft perhaps of a treatise planned on the subject. Paragraph 15 treated mathematics. "Mathematical disciplines must not be omitted, but read in the universities in an extraordinary lecture,[50] either by someone who started another course the year before, or by someone else. In private colleges, however, a philosophy instructor should do this, if convenient; otherwise someone else will explicate mathematics as much as befits the goal proposed to us. Knowledge of the *Sphere* is the absolute minimum. Ours studying academic Letters should also hear this discipline as they hear philosophy, or if this is not possible, when they hear theology. Those especially whom Superiors want to prepare for public liberal arts lectures should be trained in the discipline." Interestingly, Ledesma's short text moves from mere programmatic details to what are surely problem areas in actual teaching, the very life of the school. Two different mathematical study levels were planned. One, for all students, religious and extern, listed what he thought was the least a cultivated person should know about the topic: "Knowledge of the *Sphere* is the absolute minimum." The other level was for religious chosen to teach "liberal arts" (that is, philosophy, ethics, and mathematics), and more generally for anyone who wanted a degree. Very few Jesuits or externs took the master of arts degree; it was enough to attend the course, moving from first to final year (passing the so-called "scrutinies," that is, comprehensive evaluations in a series of question or essay tests set over the course, or in its last months), to be able to enter theology, or medicine, or law in another university. So both mathematics programs, like the others mentioned, were either incompletely taught by instructors able to teach just only a compendium, or were not completed by the students, save those with some reason: a desire to teach mathematics, or a personal interest in it.

Related to course offerings was the faculty recruitment problem. Ledesma's plans, opting to rely on expediency, precluded recruitment of specialist teachers, an inevitable consequence of the marginal position the document assigned mathematics relative to philosophy in Jesuit schools. The paragraph's first words told a good deal about the real condition of the programs: if Ledesma felt the need to urge that mathematics was not to be neglected, he intimated that neglect often occurred. The directive about the *Sphere* (that at least was studied!) clashed with the 1566 Roman College program. Yet that was a planned program, while Ledesma's remarks seem to refer to the actual practice. But no one was to do the arts program without some mathematics, as we may conclude from Ledesma's recommendation; in case it was not possible to do this in the arts program, then at least do it during the four years of theology. His last point, as the context shows, referred to smaller colleges that had no chance to found a chair of mathematics. Yet in fact, mathematics was often seen as one of many sciences that could be foregone, and so students were not held to the level of proficiency and progress set for philosophy, the true and proper course.

The Society's first years saw few mathematics chairs: in Italy up to 1590, just those at Rome and Messina; in France there were none up to 1592.[51] Notices circulated of a possible instructorship at Prague ("A lecture in mathematics will also be given, provided there are books and students.") in 1556,[52] and of one at Cologne for the teaching of the elements of mathematics, but with no professor named in the programs of 1576/77 and 1578/79.[53] At Coimbra, according to a document dated 1561/62, there was a half-hour daily mathematics lecture "in the Roman manner."[54]

Mathematics, then, not only failed to get the autonomy and prestige Nadal envisioned for it relative to philosophy, but instead tended right away to slip out of the curriculum. After the Roman College, many other colleges were established in Italy, France, Germany, Bohemia, Hungary, Spain, Portugal, Poland, and also overseas. The new schools' teaching staffs needed hundreds of masters and doctors. The Society had to provide them either by recruiting mature scholars from its ranks or by setting up teacher formation programs. And yet because of the enormous problems— financial, organizational, juridical, and political—that this tumultuous growth begot, its better men were all necessarily at work meeting the most urgent basic and immediate needs.

First of all, they needed to set up facilities and get instructors, to start basic courses. Then the *modus romanus* had to be adapted for class division and pedagogical method. Nadal was one of those who moved heaven and earth to establish Jesuit schools throughout Europe and to implement correctly the *modus romanus*.[55] Even so, despite his many commitments, he had to get involved again with the sciences he taught in Paris before he entered the Society: his help was needed to assure their integral admission into the Jesuit school programs.

3. THE WORK OF CHRISTOPHER CLAVIUS AND THE ELABORATION OF THE OFFICIAL *RATIO STUDIORUM* OF THE SOCIETY OF JESUS

Debate about mathematics teaching and the role the disciplines had relative to the other sciences and student education continued among Roman College mathematicians. Two of them, Gerolamo Torres (not Balthassar Torres, the College's first mathematics teacher) and Christopher Clavius, left notes that are invaluable for internal reconstruction of the thematic complex, in ideology and pragmatics, linked to the question of mathematics teaching. Interestingly, Nadal collaborated, or at least exchanged ideas with them, for the bottom of one of Torres' pages shows notes in Nadal's hand. The text is *De studiis mathematicis* published in *Monumenta Paedagogica* (1st ed.) along with Torres' other short note on the same topic, done in collaboration with Christopher Clavius.[56]

They treated two brief schemata for mathematics programs modeled on those of Nadal, Olave, and the *Consuetudinis*. The course should be two years, with logic and physics in the philosophy course, that is, in the first two years of the arts program. In the first schema, three months of practical arithmetic taught during the summer-autumn at the start of the academic year (August-September-October) preceded the two years. The three months led to another four or five months for Euclid and a review. The second schema wanted private readings on feast days in the third year. There were always two lectures, morning and afternoon, the first for beginners, the other for those already started.[57]

These two documents are almost the first ones, to our knowledge, entirely about mathematics. But while Torres' notes show a "technical" character, and aim to develop an optimal combination of disciplines in the mathematics course for the time allotted, Clavius' two brief texts have a quite different character and purpose; unfortunately, like Torres', they are undated. Nadal's written comments make them no later than 1580, the year he died, yet their content and tone seems to put them later, as part of the preparatory work for the first draft of the *Ratio sudiorum* that began in 1581 with Father General Claude Aquaviva's appointment of a first commission of twelve fathers.

Clavius, in fact, aimed to sell, not just explain, a plan or program. His style is discursive, and his logic precise. Study and teaching of mathematics, he argued, must not be downgraded, as happened then ("in our Society, mathematics is almost completely neglected"); there was need rather to admit the discipline's theoretical and practical value, and then work to change the situation. His arguments and proposals appeared in the 1586 *Ratio studiorum* rules for the mathematics professor, which bolsters the conjecture that he wrote them for the commission charged "to draft a plan of studies." The first of his two short texts[58] decried the gravity of the situation. Few Jesuits knew mathematics, and when the disciplines are discussed in public or private, "Ours of necessity there fall silent, with no little shame and embarrassment." This hurt the Society for it had many good practiced mathematicians. The problem's root cause lay in the schools where mathematics was little or badly studied because of poor teacher preparation and morale that in turn led to insufficient student application to the subject.

Philosophy teachers were the first to blame for devaluation of mathematics. Better that they "avoid questions that help little to understand natural phenomena, and greatly detract from the authority of mathematical disciplines among their students, like those that deny that the mathematical sciences are sciences, or have demonstrations, and claim they are abstracted from being and goodness, etc." Even that isn't enough for them; in private they steer young people away from mathematics, "as many did earlier." In truth, the philosophers don't know the basic fact that "these sciences have such close affinity to each other and to natural philosophy, that unless they help each other, they can never enhance their prestige." Without mathematics, "physics cannot be understood, especially when it treats number and the motion of celestial orbits, or the multitude of intelligences, the stars' effects that depend on their conjunctions, oppositions, and other distances between themselves, infinite division of continuous quantity, tidal ebb and flow, winds, comets, rainbows, halos and other meteorological phenomena, or ratios of motions, qualities, actions, passions, and reactions, that the *calculatores* described." The list aimed to pique the professional interest of those who taught these topics from Aristotle's books or, especially, the commentaries. Clavius raised, perhaps a bit provocatively, the question of "infinite division of continuous quantity" that marked the central Aristotelian argument against the possibility of applying mathematics to physics. But even if philosophers did not see the utility of mathematics for natural philosophy, they should consider the "examples in Aristotle, Plato, and their distinguished interpreters that are unintelligible without some knowledge of the mathematical sciences. Moreover, out of ignorance here, some philosophy professors often made egregious errors, and, even worse, published them; there are many examples." Also, philosophers should know some mathematics, at least to avoid bad syllogisms, and enough to understand Aristotle and other philosophers who treat such topics.

The first condition for "promoting mathematical sciences in Jesuit schools" was to give them a new "image." To do this, they had to educate the educators, first the philosophy professors, who molded school opinion, and then the mathematics teachers and the students. So they would not undervalue mathematical sciences, "the students must be made to realize these sciences are useful and necessary to understand correctly the rest of philosophy." He wanted the mathematics professor to be at all formal occasions, the conferral of degrees or public disputations, next to the other instructors. "This way it can easily happen that students, seeing the mathematics professor with the others at such functions, will realize that philosophy and the mathematical sciences are linked, as in fact they are." And last, "in private too, masters should encourage students to learn these disciplines, and stress their utility."

To get fully competent teachers, well motivated and ready to lecture, in mathematics was the other part of Clavius' strategy. He shared Torres' idea that public lectures could not always produce the teachers: "However, so that the Society may ever have good professors for these sciences, some members, apt and so inclined, should be selected. They can be instructed in a private academy in specialized mathematics." Keeping with this, he rejected any proposal to "read a standard topic in private," urging rather, as an asset for the Society generally, institution of a mathematics academy, private only because limited to Jesuit scholastics (those sent to the schools after their two novitiate years, in the Society's case). One last point. No one will get the master of arts degree or a doctorate in theology without examination in mathematics. The proposal confirms our suspicions about Ledesma's *De artium liberalium studiis:* for all practical purposes mathematics was optional. We can easily guess the consequences of that simple fact in a school where course marks and examinations were the biggest incentive to study, and how students viewed such proposals.

Clavius' other brief note dealt entirely with faculty problems.[59] Next to the basic need to form competent professionals was that of establishing the prestige of teaching mathematics, and then for the Society to assign fully formed men for this, not just ones who lately completed philosophy and were at most 24 years old. "It seems neither expedient, ... nor advantageous to the school, which is diminished and handicapped, that its masters are almost boys, nor for the Society's reputation that they are regularly sent to teach the more important disciplines." So it is not enough just that "those who are to profess this science are excused from teaching grammar because the year after they complete philosophy they can study mathematics in greater depth in the Jesuit house, and then for a year or two give public lectures."[60] Instead, "with philosophy completed, they should study for a whole year the topics they are to teach, as already agreed, but then attend theology, and after that teach the mathematical disciplines for the time agreed. For apart from the fact that by then they will be mature men and priests and theologians, they will honor the chair rather than embarrass it." This way no one would teach mathematics before age 30. The rest of the note analyzed in detail the advantages of the change.

Clavius' proposals merit careful study here because they were the first to see the role of mathematics in the *Ratio studiorum* as a political-cultural issue that challenged in depth Jesuit ideas and asked all school parties, students as well as teachers, for change. Change was possible only as a consequence of a political choice by Jesuit superiors. To those responsible for making and implementing such decisions, Clavius' proposals were revolutionary. They touched all key points of the question, and wanted, not partial remedies or patch work to salvage what could be salvaged, but a complex strategy able to get radical change in attitudes and structure. Clavius enjoyed great authority from his work on Gregory XIII's calendar reform, and in the polemic that swirled about that reform and involved the prestige of the Church. Clavius' work proved invaluable in that the success that accrued to the Church then also redounded to his own prestige and that of the mathematical sciences.[61]

The Gregorian calendar reform was effected in 1582. The year before, 1581, the Society's Fourth General Congregation met, and elected Claude Aquaviva to its highest office. He had a mandate to prepare the document on schools according to Ignatius' wish.

The two Clavius documents were probably done for use of the commission "ad conficiendam formulam studiorum."[62] The group completed a draft of the *Ratio* in 1585, and sent it to press the next year. Clavius' ideas and proposals were accepted for the most part in this first draft of the definitive *Ratio atque institutio studiorum*. The chapter "De Mathematicis" had a good many topics he discussed and that were reviewed here. It began with an *apologia* for mathematics: mathematics is no small help to the Society's purpose, and indispensable for all other sciences; it has infinitely many practical uses in all civil and religious life.[63] This said, it had to admit, sadly, regretfully, that the Society lacked teachers and scholars of this key material. Proposals were made on two levels: school instruction and teacher formation. If a solution is wanted for the task of preparing Jesuit scientists, the two levels must operate distinctly. A study program, like Nadal's, could not be implemented in a school whose goal was to award the doctorate in theology, not mathematics. So mathematics should be put in a special academy, a professional school, set in the Roman College: "A second professor, who could be Father Clavius, should be appointed to offer a more complete course of mathematics over a three year period, and one of the two is to explain in private to about eight or ten of Ours, who have already heard philosophy and been recruited from different provinces, and are of at least average ability and not averse to mathematics, a topic of his choice, if this is possible." The key point of Clavius' program was in this way realized. He saw its students as teachers who would foster study of mathematical sciences everywhere as a legacy of the special academy. A one-and-a-half year course in the first two years of philosophy was set for students in the normal school. Of considerable interest, and indicative of Clavius' influence, was the linking of mathematics and the *Posterior Analytics* "which can be understood only with difficulty without mathematical examples."[64]

Precise directives about lecture order came next: "Arrangements should be made that Euclid's *Elements* always gets more detailed treatment than Geography or the Sphere, especially since the latter do not require close knowledge of all Euclidean principles, but only a few of the first, that will be known after two or three months. After this, the Sphere or other more interesting such topics should be treated in the three quarters of an hour for the mathematics lecture with the first two [for Euclid], and this arrangement should be kept to the end of studies. Later, in the second year, the rest of the compendium Father Clavius will compose should be explained in the first class hour after dinner to these same auditors who are then hearing physics. When Easter comes, a second morning lecture for the benefit of new logic students should be added, where the mathematics compendium will be started anew. The same cycle is to be kept every year." This way, from mid-April until mid-June Euclid was taught; after this, and to the year's end, the Euclid lecture continued for a half hour each day, with the remaining quarter hour for the Sphere or Geography or some such topic. But what was Clavius' compendium? It should have included all the material for the mathematics course, which probably also comprised other elements of astronomy, arithmetic, algebra perhaps,[65] and physics [optics?]. No known work of the German scientist fits this description. Although the *Ratio* said Clavius would write it, very likely he never finished it, if he even started. His *Epitome of Practical Arithmetic* was a scholastic manual whose first edition, in Latin, appeared in 1585[66] at the same time as the draft of the first *Ratio*. An Italian translator, Lorenzo Castellano, in his dedication to Clavius, noted that its contents were instructional matter: "in this new translation of mine, I have recorded and fixed in memory all I know I learned from the living voice of your Reverence."[67] The booklet explained operations on integers and fractions, some elements of commercial arithmetic, for example, the "rule of three," arithmetic and geometric progressions, and square roots. It could then comprise the first part of a never completed compendium of the mathematics program material. In any event, the compendium was unfinished five years later when the second *Ratio* version, published in 1591, mentioned "a certain mathematics curriculum that Father Clavius will compose."[68]

The 1591 *Ratio* showed no shift of emphasis in what concerned mathematics from the draft of 1586. It too knew Clavius' presence. The compendium he was to prepare was cited a good three times as foundation for the course. A recommendation Clavius made in his first memorandum about the deportment of philosophy professors also got approval: they must be careful not to subvert the importance of mathematics, or to take positions denying theories it proposes, for often, in fact, the less they understand them, the greater their calumnies.[69] Even so, the ordinary course length was changed, reduced to a single year, and the half year for logic students dropped altogether. The three year special school for Jesuit scholastics became an "Academy of Mathematics," of six months length, with two daily lectures. "A knowledgeable and competent professor shall explain mathematics to Ours twice daily. They must not be involved in other studies, but devote themselves completely to lectures, repetitions, and disputations in mathematics. Those who have made great progress and are not averse to the subject, should be listed for it, to share their knowledge frequently in private academies, and in public lecture as much as need be."[70] A "lectio publica"[71] of two hours a day was also seen as a possibility, but only the physics and metaphysics students could attend it, with superiors' permission. The course program was that of the first *Ratio*, and it would stay that way in the definitive *Ratio*. Introduced for the first time were public disputations in mathematics, once a month or more, with participation of philosophers and theologians; weekly repetitions were also required. These too were kept in the definitive 1599 *Ratio*.

The 1599 *Ratio* had a succinct and dry style; its definitive form gave rules but no reasons or explanations. For mathematics, the 1599 *Ratio* took the substance of the preceding version, with three rules for the professor of mathematics: "1. He will explain Euclid's *Elements* to the physics students in a class of about three quarters of an hour. After they have been taught the *Elements* for about two months, he should introduce a bit of Geography, or the Sphere, or topics usually heard with interest. This is done along with Euclid, either on the same or alternate days. 2. Each month, or at least every other month, he should see that one of his students discusses a famous mathematics problem at a major convocation of philosophers and theologians, later there can be a disputation, if appropriate. 3. Once a month, on Saturday, the main topics explained that month should be reviewed in public, instead of a prelection" (Rules of the Mathematics Professor). And so, mathematics is here set definitively as material complementary to physics in the second year of the philosophy course. The *Ratio* gave only a simple decree about teacher formation: those apt and inclined to mathematics should be trained privately after the course.[72]

None of the three *Ratio* versions required the mathematics examination

Clavius wanted. For if mathematics were a topic for examination, it would no longer have complementary status. An appropriate chair would have to be founded in any college that offered advanced instruction. But we know that was never the case; only the largest colleges had mathematics chairs. At the end of the sixteenth century these chairs at last began to be common in the Society, as its scholastic organization left an experimental period to enter a phase of structure consolidation. In the seventeenth century, many Jesuit colleges worldwide offered mathematics instruction, the role of which in the plan of studies was now clear. Mathematics complemented the philosophy course, and because of its obvious affinity with physics, was always scheduled along with it, as the *Ratio studiorum* prescribed.

NOTES

1. MHSI (=*Monumenta Paedagogica Societatis Iesu,* edited, completely revised, and augmented with new texts by Ladislaus Lukacs, S.I., I (1540-1556), Rome, 1965, p. 271. We cite this edition as *Mon. Paed. 1965.* The earlier edition, *Monumenta Paedagogica Societatis Iesu quae primam Rationem studiorum anno 1586 editam praecessere,* Madrid, 1901, will be cited as *Mon. Paed. 1901.*

2. C. 12: *De scientiis quae tradendae sunt in universitatibus Societatis;* c. 13: *De modo et ordine praedictas facultates tractandi;* c 14: *De libris qui praelegendi sunt;* c 15: *De cursibus et gradibus.* The official text of the *Constitutions* was that published in 1583 *(Constitutiones Societatis Iesu cum earum declarationibus,* Roma) by decree of the Order's Fourth General Congregation, held between February and April of 1581. The *Constitutions* are divided in parts (indicated by p. followed by a Roman numeral) and paragraphs (c. followed by an Arabic numeral). "Declarations" are attached to every chapter (indicated by d. followed by a capital letter); St. Ignatius was their author, and they have the same legal authority as the text.

3. *Const.,* p. IV, c. 7, d. B. But he also asserted that "they may however be started in the more important disciplines for the benefit of the places where the colleges are located, always keeping in mind what is more pleasing to God" (*Const.,* p. IV, c. 7, p. 1).

4. "In the Declarations, letter A, of topics that are to be read in the colleges, this has not been observed, nor is it observed in many colleges where the Arts are read . . . but I think it should be observed, as far as possible" (*"Quaedam ex Constitutionibus quae non observantur, inter quae multa sunt etiam quae forte non expedit observari"* in *Congr.* 20, a. 76, n. 46). ·

   See, in turn, the opinion of Jerome Nadal, one of the leaders in the Society's first few years: "However it will not be out of place, and even useful, where college resources and student size allow, that the teaching of liberal arts, and at times of theology, be done there too, just as in the Roman College" (G. Nadal, *Scholia in Constitutiones* 336-7). In fact, even at first with Ignatius still alive, what determined whether or not a college had higher courses was hard data like "college resources" and "student numbers," that were reviewed from time to time. As a result, conflicts with local universities arose; the most notable and raucous was that with Padua, where, on 23 December 1591, a Venetian Senate decree ordered the Jesuits to stop public teaching, and do so only in private among themselves.

5. *Const.*, p. IV, c. 13, d. A.

6. P. I. de Polanco, *Chronicon*, 1548, 213: "Father Nadal indeed instituted three readers of grammar . . . Martin Isadore for dialectic, Andreas Frusius for Greek literature, and Father Nadal himself for Hebrew; however he left the prelections to Father Andreas. He himself, though marked for college administration, taught scholastic theology in the morning, and Cases of Conscience after dinner."

7. Jerome Nadal was born on 11 August 1507 at Palma de Majorca. After finishing studies at Paris, he was recruited for the Society by St. Ignatius in 1545. He resided at the College of Messina from 1548 to 1552. Recalled to Rome in 1553, he was sent to Spain and Portugal to promulgate the *Constitutions*. Later he was visitor in all the European provinces, rector of the Roman College, and Vicar General. He died at Rome in 1580.

8. Polanco, *Chronicon*, 1548, 214: "After the schools opened, they published their laws and constitutions which were approved and put into effect."

9. *Mon. Paed. 1965*, p. 26.

10. Published respectively at Paris in 1535 and 1542, at Oppenheim in 1512, and at Vienna in 1542.

11. "Most of all, Master Nadal, who came as reader in scholastic theology, is well versed in this, in Scripture, and in dogmatic (theology); he knows the decrees and the councils. He is also learned in mathematics, which he read in Paris (as I believe you know), and quite diligent at it. He is equally versed in the arts and humane letters, Latin, Greek, and Hebrew, as you may have seen" (MHSI, *Monumenta Ignatiana*, Series prima, *Sancti Ignatii de Loyola epistolae et instructiones*, I-XII, Madrid, 1919, II, 25-26).

12. *Chronicon*, 1549, 350: "At that time (autumn resumption of studies) Father Andreas Frusius also offered a lecture in dialectics (which was to be done yearly in the philosophy course), with good results, until he had a successor. For in the second year Master Isadore was teaching natural philosophy . . . Father Nadal himself had three different lectures, to wit, Euclid in mathematics, and other authors in Greek and Hebrew literature." The mathematics lectures had gratifying success with no fewer auditors than the lectures in the higher courses: "So in November Father Nadal

himself noted there were sixteen students in dialectics, thirteen in philosophy, ten in his Greek lecture, three or four in Hebrew, and ten or twelve in mathematics." Only three or four students heard scholastic theology since few externs were ready for these lectures, and the religious "were not yet coming to our schools."

13. The *Constitutions* also anticipated the "public school" in special cases: "Prudence will determine whether apart from ordinary instructors who should know well their auditors, there should be one or more who like public professors will read philosophy, mathematical sciences, or other disciplines, with greater resources than ordinary readers, according to circumstances of places and persons with whom they deal, keeping in mind greater edification and service of God" (*Const.*, p. IV, c. 13, d. C).

14. *Mon. Paed* 1965, pp. 148-49.

15. Johann Regiomontanus, *De triangulis omnimodis libri V*, Venezia, 1533; I. Nemorarius, *Geometria vel de triangulis libri IV*, in *Opera*, Paris, 1514.

16. *Mon. Paed.* 1965, pp. 149-50.

17. Johann Regiomontanus, *Epitome in Ptolemaei magnam compositionem*, Basel, 1543.

18. G. Peurbach, *Theoricae novae planetarum*, 2nd ed., Wittenberg, 1553, ff. 20-21.

19. Nuremberg, 1535.

20. Paris, 1500.

21. *Mon Paed.* 1965, pp. 147-48.

22. Ibid., p. 148.

23. Ibid., p. 393. The "printed list" Jay wanted was made at Messina in 1548 early in the academic year 1548-49, and printed at the Messina press of Pietro Spira. It announced courses to be offered (languages, arts, theology); mathematics was not listed. Teaching methods used were given only as "disputations and other ways to get results" along with "good exercises, acts, and disputations, according to Parisian practice" (*Mon. Paed.* 1965, pp. 383-86).

24. The *modus parisiensis* or "Parisian method" was devised at the University of Paris, renowned for its theology faculty, for which its arts faculty (philosophy) was the preparation. But its didactic methods more than its intellectual orientation won the approval of Ignatius and adoption first by Nadal at Messina, and then by Jesuit schools ever afterward. The Parisian method (developed by the theology faculty

and its associated colleges, Sorbonne, Montaigu, and St. Barbara) "had the following distinctive characteristics: 1. The students of a discipline were usually divided into classes by age and accomplishment ('senior,' 'more advanced,' 'elementary'). 2. The students were not allowed to attend at will the lectures of other professors. 3. Repetitions and public disputations were regularly scheduled. 4. While Italian instructors were preoccupied with delivering public lectures in a scholarly way, the Parisians kept close to their students, paying careful attention to their personal development" (R. G. Villoslada, *Storia del Collegio Romano dal suo inizio [1551] alla soppressione della Compania di Gesù* [1773], Rome, 1954, p. 11).

25. *Mon. Paed.* 1965, pp. 24,* 163-64.

26. "The entire course in Aristotle will be done in three years" (*Mon. Paed.* 1965, p. 177).

27. Ibid., p. 166. The philosophy course instead was described in detail, with a prescribed reading list.

28. "After the first half year [of the philosophy course, without mathematics study] . . . they will hear the mathematics lecture in the third hour which will always be one hour before dinner . . . . After a year-and-a-half the students may hear the mathematics lecture read in the morning, and the other mathematics lecture usually read an hour after dinner" (*Mon. Paed.* 1965, pp. 176-77).

29. Francesco Maurolyco began to read mathematics in the Jesuit College of Messina in the academic year 1569-70. He was aware of Roman College practice, thanks to Father Balthassar Torres. Another Torres, like him a Roman College mathematician and philosophy teacher, developed two brief mathematics programs, in which Maurolyco figured among the authors read. See M. Scaduto, "Il matematico Francesco Maurolico e i gesuiti," *Archivum Historicum Societatis Iesu* 18 (1949), pp. 126-41. For the mathematics programs of Gerolamo Torres, cf. infra.

30. "The most important university event of that era in France, and one that revealed clearly the different mindsets, was the foundation of the Collège de France. This was the work of Francis I and his great adviser, William Budé . . . . Far from wanting to create an institutional rival for the University, Francis I simply named professors 'King's Readers in the University of Paris,' six in all, three for Hebrew, two for Greek, one for mathematics. The Sorbonne tried to destroy the royal foundation, . . . as Noël Beda said: although it had no desire

to impede reading Greek and Hebrew literature, the learning and doctrine of which it honored, it feared most of all that language professors not theologically literate would damage or derogate the translation of Sacred Scripture" (S. d'Irsay, *Histoire des universitès françaises et étrangères dès origenes à nous jours*, 2 vols., Paris, 1933, I, pp. 270-73.)

31. Since language instruction was entrusted to Jesuit professors who had to be doctors in theology, the Sorbonne's objections as Noël Beda expressed them (see note 30), began to subside. Significant in any case was the way the Society faced problems by trying to resolve them at the appropriate points. Avoidable counter-productive negative approaches were not its style.

32. *Const*, p. IV, c. 7, d. C. This chapter was written with those on the universities, i.e., it dated to 1553-54.

32.bis *Const.*, p. IV, c. 12, d. C.

33. "The doctrine the Society's scholastics should study," p. IV, cap. 5, p. 1.

34. Absence of mathematics from the list does not imply that Ignatius did not want the Society's scholastics to study it. From the 1556 *Constitutions for the Scholastics of the Society of Jesus at Padua*, which Ignatius wrote with the help of Laínez (*Mon. Paed. 1965,* pp. 3-5), we learn how the first Jesuit scholastics, sent to study at the University of Padua, were to devote themselves to the arts course, and also to mathematics: "The other two-and-a-half years (of the arts course) are for natural philosophy, metaphysics, mathematics, and moral philosophy, as the lecture schedule allows" (ibid., p. 11.)

34bis. C. 12, p. 1.

34ter. C. 12, p. 2 and 3.

35. C. 14, p. 3. The term "metaphysics" was added by the First General Congregation of 1558. Ignatius, in fact, had not put it in the philosophy course, in contrast to Nadal, Olave, and constant later practice. In the Roman College "metaphysics is read in the triennium for logic, natural and moral philosophy, and the mathematical arts (as much as is necessary)" (Polanco's letter to Adriaenssens, 24 October 1553, in *Mon. Paed. 1965,* p. 443). Polanco's letter spells out class order in the philosophy curriculum: "The first class in the elements of dialectics, the second in the more advanced books of logic, the third class started in the books 'de physico auditu,' following Parisian methods, and that of Louvain."

Polanco confirmed that Ignatius himself approved this to fix regulation of the philosophy curriculum: "Father Ignatius however set the philosophy course at three years" (*Chronicon*, 1553, 8).

36. *Mon. Paed. 1965*, p. 437.

37. But remember that the doctrinal justification lay in the fact that Jesuit schools were primarily "professional" schools for Jesuits and secular priests, to form theologians only. Only from a modern viewpoint can we consider the public service role as foremost, which in effect they did in growing measure. But the schools were, first of all, in a special way in this initial period, an instrument for renovation of the Church.

38. P. Ioannes de Polanco, S.I., *Industriae quibus iuvetur Societas ad finem sibi propositum assequendum* (Means to help the Society attain the goal proposed), in *Mon. Paed. 1965*, p. 34.

39. "Those with more time and talent may study Greek and other humanities such as rhetoric, poetry, history, and cosmography..." (ibid., p. 33).

40. Such were those of the missions and colleges outside Europe, in India, China, and South America. In China, for example, the mathematical sciences were among the most important ways to come in contact with the local community, and to begin conversion and instruction: see P. D'Elia, *Galileo in Cina. Relazioni attraverso il Collegio Romano tra Galileo e i Gesuiti scienziati missionari in Cina: 1610-1640*, Roma, 1947. But more generally, the universal scope of Jesuit work (outside Europe, but also in the Reformation lands, especially Germany) always had a remarkable inner tendency to new approaches, and to consider ideas not entirely orthodox.

40bis. The clearest and most precise statement of Bellarmine's opinion on the matter occurs in his famous reply to Foscarini of 12 April 1615, published in the Edizione Nazionale of the *Opere di Galileo Galilei*, 2nd ed., Florence, 1929-1939, vol. XII, pp. 171-72.

41. F. Charmot, *La pédagogie des Jesuites, ses principes, son actualité* Paris, 1951, p. 472.

42. Letter of Juan de Polanco to Jean Pelletier, rector of the College of Ferrara, from Rome, 21 September 1555, in *Mon Paed. 1965*, pp. 457-63. His letter recounted the status of Roman College teaching: "From the start, things have always grown, and now all faculties are represented, save medicine and law. The staff has hardworking and learned masters. Eight or nine teach Latin, Greek, and Hebrew.

Five lecture in liberal arts and philosophy. Apart from the three regular courses, there are two extraordinary lecturers, one for natural philosophy, the other for mathematics, so that in three years an appropriate amount of the disciplines can be heard for theology." As for Roman College internationalism, he provided data both about student origins: "some came to our college in Rome (which they knew by reputation), others to the German College, from upper and lower Germany, Austria, Bohemia, Moravia, Silesia, Slovenia, Denmark, Gotha, Ireland and England," and about the effects its founding already had in fostering like ventures: "the college is international in another way too: from its foundation sprang many other colleges in Italy and elsewhere, as Your Reverence knows, and, as reported, thanks to it, each year colonies can be sent to lands that ask for them, such as Argentina,... Ratisbon, Prussia, and many others."

43. The university chapters of the *Constitutions* came some months after the rule of studies Ignatius wanted for the Roman College. Some modifications by Ignatius left them on the same study level Nadal and Olave proposed. The most important ones looked to removing metaphysics from the faculty of arts (Polanco, *Chronicon*, 1553, 7: "Three arts courses have been started together: first, dialectics from the beginning, the second on the deeper parts of Aristotle's logic and ethics, the third in physics."), which was to be three-and-a-half years (Polanco to Adriaenssens, *Mon. Paed. 1965*, p. 443: "Candidates should be promoted to the teaching office if they are found well qualified to teach after a half year for examinations and responses, but not otherwise"). Other changes looked to redimensioning the mathematics programs and the institution of the biennium of repetitions and exercises after the four-year theology course, first of the laureates. Later, metaphysics was returned to the faculty of arts, and the First General Congregation, in 1558, wanted it mentioned in the *Constitutions* (p. IV, c. 14, p. 3: "In logic, natural and moral philosophy, and metaphysics, the doctrine of Aristotle is to be followed").

44. Reported in G. M. Pachtler, S.I., *Ratio studiorum et institutiones scholasticae Societatis Iesu per Germaniam olim vigentes* I-IV, Berlin 1887-1894, I, pp. 192-97. Pachtler reproduces the text of a manuscript in the Archives of the Society's Upper German Province; the manuscript is entitled *Gubernatio Collegii Romani ac*

1mo in literis et spiritualibus. Anno 1565. Villoslada, in his *Storia del Collegio Romano*, cites extensively from the *Consuetudines Collegii Romani*, a manuscript in the Gregorian University Archives, the content of which coincides exactly with that published by Pachtler. For this reason, the *Consuetudines* should be dated back to 1566 at least, being the original from which at least that copy would have been taken, and not to shortly before 1574, as Villoslada supposed. We may also suppose that more copies of the document were made and sent to the various provinces insofar as it had a model for school organization. The *Consuetudines* were also published from another codex in *Mon. Paed. 1901*, pp. 464-70.

45. The single difference of note, relative to the definitive systemization, was the length of the course, again three-and-a-half years.

46. *Constitutiones tam commodae aptaeque quem sanctae Almae Salmatinensis Academiae toto terrarum orbe florentissimae* (*The commodious and useful Constitutions of the cherished and holy Academy of Salamanca*) Salamanca, 1562, quoted from S. d'Irsay, *Histoire des universités françaises* I, p. 334, note 6.

47. Father James Ledesma was professor of theology in the Roman College from 1556 to 1562, and prefect of studies from 1563 to 1575.

48. *Mon. Paed 1901*, pp. 338-453.

49. Ibid., pp. 460 ff. This was written for use by all the Society's schools, not for the Roman College alone.

50. The 1548 *Constitutiones Collegii Messanensis* state "he will read mathematics *extra ordinem*," like the Roman College, "there are two extraordinary readers, one for natural philosophy, the other for mathematics" (Polanco to Adriaenssens, *op. cit.*).

51. Cf. F. de Dainville, S.I., "L'Enseignement des mathématiques dans les Collèges Jésuites de France du XVIᵉ au XVIIIᵉ siècle," *Revue d'histoire des sciences et leurs applications*, 7, nn. 1-2 (January-June 1954) pp. 6-21, 102-23. The second part of the paper in no. 2 of 1954 has a table of the mathematics chairs in France from the Society's origin to its suppression. The first known chair is that of the Collège of Pont-à-Mousson, probably in 1592.

52. *Ordo lectiomum quae in Collegto Regio apud S. Clementem ad J. Christi gloriam et utilitatem publicam instituentur atque continuabuntur* (*Order of lectures that are scheduled for the Royal College at St. Clements to the glory of Jesus Christ and the public*

utility and which will be continued), printed in Pachtler, *op. cit.,* I, pp. 150 ff. The problem of books and instructional aids persisted, especially in mathematics and astronomy instruction. Books on these topics were less common and accessible in the schools than philosophy texts. Instruments were also needed, at least compass, quadrant, and astrolabe. See B. Salino's letter to Christopher Clavius from Genoa, 14 January 1605, where he bemoaned the college's lack of books and instruments "because the science was never at any time read here." He told Clavius his dire need, listing some texts and requesting compass, quadrant, and astrolabe. (Pontifical Gregorian University Archives, 529 [Clavius II], 181). For the instruments used, or at least the proper use of which was explained to students, see also the table in Gerolamo Torres' two brief texts at p. 21.

53. *Catalogus lectionum Gymnasii Coloniensis toto anno observandus, a Calendis Novembris anni 1576 usque ad Calendas Novembris sequentis anni 1577 (Catalog of Lectures in the Cologne Gymnasium to be held in the entire year from the Calends of November 1576 to Calends of November of the following year 1577);* the second document has instead the catalog of lectures from November 1578 to November 1579. Both are in Pachtler, *op. cit.,* p. 230-35. The first catalog prescribed for the physics class that "In the first hour, a topic in mathematics is read, e.g., in the first semester, the *Sphere* of John of Sacrobosco," in the second semester Aristotle's *Ethics* will be read. There were two instructors for these classes: Father Andreas Vermadius, who read Aristotle's *Physics*, mathematics, and the *Ethics*. Also, he presided at the "Repetitions" and the "Disputations." Father Bolandus read the *De caelo*, the *Meteorologica*, the *De generatione et corruptione* [in the ms. *de ortu atque interitu*]. He also read the last lecture with another, in the metaphysics class. Two years later (1578-79) mathematics was detached from the true and proper program; Fr. Bolandus read it at the "First Hour on Holy Days," perhaps because Andreas Vernadius, who read the *Sphere* of Sacrobosco, was no longer an instructor.

54. "See to it that mathematics is read a half hour each day according to Roman practice" (*De scholis artium. De las artes* in *Mon. Paed. 1901*, p. 673).

55. Nadal's life, better than anyone else's, reflected the rapid pace of development in these years, as well as the number and size of the problems Jesuits faced. In 1553, no longer rector of the College of

Messina, Nadal went to Spain and Portugal to promulgate the *Constitutions.* There he visited the colleges of Barcelona, Valencia, Alcalá, Saragossa, Cordova, Ebora, Coimbra, and some others. In 1555 he met the Emperor in Germany and arranged the foundation of the College of Prague. Afterwards he visited the colleges of Dillingen, Ingolstadt, and Vienna where he stayed for a long time. After a return to Rome, he visited the colleges of Venice, Padua, Ferrara, Bologna, Modena, Genoa, and Florence. In late 1555, he returned to Spain to visit the colleges of Alicante, Valencia, Valladolid, and some others. After a stay at Rome for the death of Ignatius and the First General Congregation, he resumed visiting Europe, from Portugal to the Netherlands to Germany. Everywhere he gave instructions, advice, direction. After a brief stint as Superintendent of the Roman College, he was sent back to Germany in 1566. There he again visited the colleges at Munich, Ingolstadt, Dillingen, and Vienna. Then he went to Tirnau, Olmutz, and again in Hungary to Presburg and Kremnitz. He moved into Poland, where he gave new instructors to the colleges of Braunnsberg and Poltava. He also visited the College of Prague, and went about Renania. In Flanders he was busy at the colleges of Louvain, Liege, Antwerp, Douai, and Dinant. Nadal was next in France, at the colleges of Paris, Verdun, Cambrai, Lyons. He was then Vicar General for 15 months until Everard Mercurian was elected General in 1573. He approved the two universities of Milan and Lorraine, and promised foundation of the College of Fulda. After the election of Mercurian, his activity stopped. He stayed at Rome, then at Hall, near Innsbruck. From there he returned to Rome, where he died on 3 April 1580.

56. The second paper is entitled "De rebus mathematicis"; both were already published in *Mon. Paed. 1901,* pp. 477-78.

57. For this, see Olave, *op. cit.,* p. 177: "After a year and a half, the students may hear the mathematics lecture read in the morning, and then hear the other mathematics lecture ordinarily read an hour after dinner."

58. *Modus quo disciplinae mathematicae in scholis Societatis possint promoveri* in *Mon. Paed. 1901,* pp. 471-74. Since they are undated, "first" refers to the order of publication in the *Mon. Paed. 1901.*

59. *De re mathematica instructio* in *Mon. Paed. 1901,* pp. 474-76. The *Monumenta* editors supplied the title.

60. Such a norm was already known the year before the draft of this

document, seemingly in the Roman College ("It was enacted the year before that...").

61. The 1586 *Ratio* explicitly refers to calendar reform: "At Rome also, save for a person or two, there is hardly anyone who can teach these disciplines, or is available to the Apostolic See for a discussion of Ecclesiastical time" (*De mathematicis* 1).

62. The *Ratio* had three editions. The first, in 1586, composed by a committee of six priests, was sent to all the Order's provinces for comments to be returned to Rome. A second draft, formulated on the basis of these responses, was published in 1591. Its discursive and analytic style made it more an essay than a code. So a third and final *Ratio* was prepared, sent to press at the end of 1598, and published in 1599. The final text was much more concise and arid in its preceptive form than its predecessors. The Seventh General Congregation (1615) made some mild changes for a new edition in 1616 that was not further altered, and finally always entered into the *Institutum Societatis Iesu* in that form. Cf. *La Ratio studiorum e la parte quarta delle Constitutioni della Compagnia di Gesù*, edited by M. Barbera, Padua, 1942, pp. 41-46.

63. "These (mathematical arts give) poets, historians, logicians, and natural philosophers demonstration paradigms; (they provide) civil rulers with admirable domestic and military administration techniques; physicists with the types and criteria of celestial orbits, light, colors, transparent media, and sounds; metaphysicians with the number of spheres and intelligences; theologians with special aspects of divine creation; and all this plus spin off from the mathematicians' work that benefits public health, transportation, and agriculture."

64. "(The professor of mathematics) is to offer a short course in mathematics with daily lectures for a year and a half that both Ours and extems are to attend. He will begin this course after the Resurrection Pasch, first in the morning at the school hour set for logic students, who are then preparing for the *Posterior Analytics* which can hardly be understood without mathematical examples."

65. Clavius wrote an algebra text published however only in 1608: *Algebra Christofori Clavii Bambergensis e Societate Iesu*, Roma, apud Bartholomaeum Zannettum, 1608.

66. Christofori Clavii Bambergeosis e Soc. Iesu, *Epitome Arithmeticae Practicae nunc denuo ab ipso auctore recognita*, Roma, Dominicus Basa, 1585.

67. *Arithmetica prattica composta dal molto Rev. Padre Christoforo Clavio Bambergense della Compagnia di Gesù et tradotta da latino in italiano dal Signor Lorenzo Castellano Patrizio Romano*, Roma, Domenico Basa, 1586. The preface provides great insight into the Roman College mathematician's viewpoint on his science. To quote the most significant passages from the Latin edition (1585): "Without Arithmetic, as I see it, no science, as Plato claimed [in marg. *Epinomis*] or human society can survive. Plato said forthrightly [in *Epinomis* and *Republic* VII] that to remove Arithmetic from life is to take prudence and all restraint from the world, for without it neither public nor private domain can stand. In fact, other disciplines so depend on Arithmetic that its collapse would take them with it. For, without mastery of the entire number realm, neither astrologer nor geometer will stand open testing that his theorems show truth and beauty linked with utility; for should even the least fault appear in the ideas considered, you would see utter ruin of the rest. And so Plato, Prince of Reason, [in *Republic* VII] wanted it as entrance and vestibule to all other sciences, not just because they are nothing without numbers, but because the mind comes alive working with numbers, and is readied for all other learning."

68. *Regulae professoris mathematicae*, 4.

69. "Let authorities take special care lest in their teaching the philosophy professors either negate the prestige of mathematics, or subvert its ideas, like those about epicycles, for often the less one knows about a topic, the more he demeans it" (*Rules of the Provincial, De mathematicis* 44).

70. Ibid., 41.

71. For "lectio publica," see note 13 above.

72. Preparation of specialists in the mathematical sciences was then done outside the official studies curriculum. Galileo's adversary Horazio Grassi (Lothario Sarsi Sigensano) is a good example. He was Roman College mathematics professor from 1616 to 1628 (with a two year hiatus from 1624 to 1626). As a Roman College student, he was assigned to mathematics just for the full scholastic year 1605-1606, after he completed the philosophy curriculum but before he began the university theology course. (See C. Costantini, *Baliani e i gesuiti*, Florence, 1969, pp. 71-72).

Mathematics Instruction in Jesuit Colleges of Northern Italy

Giuseppe Cosentino

The new physical world vision consequent on the seventeenth-century scientific revolution won tenure in school programs only in the nineteenth century. Yet even before that, mathematics instruction assured the presence in the life of the old curricula of new ideas, or at least treatment of terrestrial and celestial physics procedures with mathematical methods. This was surely true in Jesuit schools, where mathematics courses comprised not only arithmetic, geometry, and algebra, but also diverse use of mensuration and calculus in astronomy and astrology, computation of time (calendar and sundial), surveying, theory of music, optics (perspective), and mechanics.

We know Jesuit college study patterns followed the *modus parisiensis*.[1] The Society not only adopted University of Paris pedagogy, but instructional programs, and their content had it also as their model.[2] In contrast to Italian universities, the University of Paris had four faculties: arts (philosophy), medicine, law, and theology; the first was preparation for the others.[3] The three-year Jesuit college arts course led to the subsequent study of theology, and was in substance a course of Aristotelian philosophy, distributed over logic (1st year), natural philosophy or physics (2nd year), and metaphysics (3rd year). Some auxiliary disciplines were included, for example, moral philosophy (in 1st year, with logic), and mathematics (in 2nd year, with physics).

Antagonism between the mathematical disciplines and the core philosophical and theological curricula was felt, if nowhere else, in the task of fully integrating the former into an Aristotelian system of sciences that assigned mathematics a more practical than theoretical role, and tended to admit, if not really honor, its utility, rather than its intrinsic noetic value. Mathematical progress, in contrast, was closely linked with the rise of a new scientific outlook frankly critical of the assumptions and traditional methods of physics and Aristotelian cosmology. Hence an antagonism, not open at first, developed by the second half of the sixteenth century into a more or less explicit confrontation. In the circumstances the Society's

81

adoption of a precise, nuanced commitment in the field of mathematical disciplines, despite its substantially conservative thrust, represented a significant choice for a cultural policy of "accommodation," that is, availability for a meeting (that could become collaboration) with the innovative tendencies of European scientific thought.

In the sixteenth century the new science could, in general, grow beside the old qualitative physics, and was often inextricably linked with it. This difficult, though not always impossible, co-existence strengthened the conciliatory and moderate tendencies of the Jesuit scientists, who in the next century amid mounting difficulties carried out programs that in truth became ever less credible and effective for mediation between the old and the new. Jesuit school interest in mathematics was countered by the established primacy of Aristotelian physics, and because the tension and ambiguity connected with such co-presence was not resolved by open debate between the two sides, an increasingly detailed series of rules came to delimit the respective tasks and functions of the teachers and scholars of philosophy and mathematics. The history of Jesuit college and university mathematics instruction is, then, of great interest for a more precise historiographic (and not just ideological) reconstruction of the history of science in the critical period of the seventeenth and eighteenth centuries.

After founding the first colleges for externs, Ignatius accepted the fact that the Society of Jesus was becoming a teaching order. But if the Society was to go that way to fulfill its foundational mission, he had to reaffirm the goal of all Society works, keeping means and ends distinct: "So also, since the arts and natural sciences dispose the mind to theology, and help perfect its knowledge and use, and these in themselves help to the same end, they are to be taught with appropriate diligence and by competent instructors, sincerely seeking in everything the honor and glory of God."[4] According to a venerable tradition, the best scientific system to prepare "the mind . . . for theology" was Aristotle's: "In logic, natural and moral philosophy, and metaphysics, Aristotle's doctrine should be followed."[5] That was the method the universities in Paris, Padua, and Bologna, the age's key cultural centers, used, each in its own way.

All the same, some Jesuit voices spoke for the other side. Among the most authoritative and powerful was that of Christopher Clavius, whose work was decisive for curriculum development in the colleges. According to him, mathematics was not just useful, but indispensable for natural philosophy ("natural philosophy is hobbled and incomplete without the mathematical disciplines"). He urged symbiosis of the two disciplines.

Such accord and mutual support could be realized in the colleges only if mathematics enjoyed the same respect as philosophy: "Secondly, students must realize that the mathematical sciences are useful and necessary for correct understanding of the rest of philosophy, and a great asset toward perfect erudition in all the other arts. In fact, mathematics and natural philosophy have such affinity that unless they help each other, they cannot maintain their status. It will be a big step up if philosophy teachers avoid topics that help little to probe nature but only derogate the mathematical sciences among their hearers, e.g., claims that the mathematical disciplines are not sciences, do not have demonstrations, and only abstract from being and goodness, etc."[6]

Clavius attended to the work of teacher formation: "So that the Society may always have competent professors for these disciplines, some apt and able men should be set aside for them, and instructed in the various mathematical disciplines in a private academy. Otherwise it seems impossible that such studies can long survive in the Society or be fostered there."[7] Through Clavius' influence, the definitive *Ratio studiorum (1599)*, although setting a decisively subordinate role for mathematics in keeping it to a one year course and as a complement to physics, did arrange that interested students could attend private lectures after the course.[8] Clavius himself founded a school and a Roman College scientific tradition that for decades formed many of the Society's most renowned scientists and teachers. Thanks to a courageous group of scholars, mathematics was properly fostered in the Society of Jesus, and routinely taught in its colleges. From the very beginning, the Society's ranks boasted distinguished scientists and extern colleagues too, for example, Francesco Maurolyco, who taught in the college of Messina in the scholastic year 1569-70.[9]

At the end of the sixteenth century the colleges continued to grow in number and importance. After the first "experiments" of the decade 1540-50 (Goa, Gandia, Messina) opened the way for an unexpected apostolate, the years right after the Roman College foundation (1551) became an era of feverish activity that swept away every obstacle and hesitation. Teaching became the Society's principal apostolate, and its pedagogy enjoyed brilliant, unanticipated success. Heirs of a medieval university culture, the Jesuit colleges embedded that legacy in a centralized organization to provide uniformity of cultural content. The *Ratio studiorum* was the single guide that regulated Jesuit colleges worldwide, and evaluated their instructional methods for efficiency and practicality.

Like the universities, that, ever less at the center of current science, gradually lost their traditional high-level research roles, and like the academies, then characteristic centers of modern age science, the Jesuit colleges were co-opted as centers of activity in the making of the modern world.[10] Until now historians have attended almost exclusively to the Jesuit scholars' own contributions to the development of scientific knowledge, or, occasionally, to the Order's policies in various controversies, in the Galileo case, for example. There are, however, no systematic studies of the Jesuit colleges that effected and transmitted the Society's cultural values. Nor are there precise indications and data about the effective quantitative and qualitative consistency of mathematics teaching within these institutions. This is a big gap, given the characteristically collaborative and progressive nature of modern science after the seventeenth-century revolution, and the fundamental role that institutional organization of research and its liaison with civil society, or its more educated part and ruling class at least, had from then on.

Apart from general histories of the Society, those that study the various provinces[11] neither provide adequate data about collegiate instruction in general or about mathematics instruction in particular; they relate almost exclusively the external events of the colleges. The few works known that look explicitly at Jesuit college mathematics instruction are those of De Dainville.[12] Data about mathematics instruction also appear in R G. Villoslada's *Storia del Collegio Romano, dal suo inizio (1551) alla soppressione della Compagnia di Gesù (1773)*.[13] *M*. Scaduto's fine paper, "Le origini dell'Università di Messina (a proposito del quarto centenario)"[14] discusses Nadal's mathematics program and teaching in the college of Messina. Note too Scaduto's paper (see note 9) on the famous mathematician Francesco Maurolyco's link to the Messina college.

Northern Italian Jesuit colleges have received no better attention, though the Domus Galilaeanà program has recently given priority to their history. Del Monti's work on the Turin province, already noted, records events for the colleges of Genoa and Turin. Some data about Brera and the Collegio dei Nobili at Brescia can be found in the Treccani Foundation city histories of Milan and Brescia. Useful notes for the history of mathematics instruction at Genoa during the first half of the 1600s are found in C. Costantini's *Baliani e i gesuiti*[15] that sketches events about the Jesuit college chair of mathematics.

Indeed, the colleges and the universities of Bologna, Parma, Genoa, and Milan, along with the Roman College, were the key centers for the events we tried to sketch. Many famous Jesuit scientists worked in northern Italy: in the 1600s, De Dominis, Cabei, Riccioli, F. M. Grimaldi, Lana Terzi, Tommaso Ceva; in the 1700's, Saccheri, Riccati, and Boscovich, the founder of Brera's astronomical observatory. But this list of great names, needed to provide coherence and prestige to the cultural phenomenon, should also help construct a full network of peer contacts between scholars inside and outside the Society doing advanced scientific research and its analysis, contacts that existed in the colleges and especially in the chairs of mathematics that were their natural organizational centers.

To reconstruct the history and characteristics of mathematics instruction in northern Italian Jesuit schools we need to set up a data bank identifying archives and their basic organizations. Happily, there are copious sources for the colleges, concentrated in good part in the general archives of the Society of Jesus.

The archives of the General's Curia received all the different reports that house, college, and novitiate superiors were supposed to do periodically to give the Society's government data and information useful for governance.[16] The general archives have in fact three divisions, but only the first two that house documents for the old Society up to the Suppression (1773), are of interest for us. These two sources, housed together, have, however, different origins and contents, and so were not combined, but keep their own document organization.[17] The Fondo Gesuitico does not concern us, but the Archivum Romanum Societatis Iesu (ARSI) holds the documents directly useful for college histories.

The first sources to examine are the "triennial" and "short (or annual)" catalogs. The names describe the time intervals between one report and the next, but the catalogs took definitive form only with the norms that Superior General Claude Acquaviva promulgated. He amplified the *formula scribendi* that his predecessor Eduardo Mercurian sent to the provinces in 1578.[18] The catalogs were to be compiled by college rectors and house prefects, and sent to the provincial, who in turn would send them to Rome for an archival amanuensis to copy into the appropriate books.

The annual catalogs supply data for histories of the chairs because they list, college by college, the Jesuits and their offices that year. This way one can make a table of mathematics instructors, year by year, with the teachers' names. ARSI has the *catalogi breves* of the Venetian province from the scholastic year 1613-14, and those of the Milan province from 1614-15, in unbroken sequence up to 1773.[19] The triennial catalogs, in turn, are most important for their biographical data, and are divided into a first, second, and third catalog. The first two treat personnel only, and provide brief biographical sketches: age, place of birth, entrance into the Society, studies completed, offices held and grade in the Society (first catalog); the second catalog lists superiors' evaluations of their subjects' intellectual and moral capacities, and their attitudes.[20] The third catalog tried to provide a succinct statistical table of the status of the college (or house) in the form of a brief report about instruction and economic conditions (revenue, debts, etc.).[21] Where annual reports are deficient, triennial catalogs can also help by way of conjecture to establish the presence or absence of some programs. We rely especially on triennial catalogs for the period from 1598-90 to the start of the unbroken sequence of annual catalogs; thanks to them we can make a table, clear if incomplete, of the chairs of mathematics at the time.[22]

Even for the preceding period there are some "extraordinary" documents with precise data, such as the *Short Catalog of the Venetian Province in the year 1582, on the occasion of Visitation*[23] that lists the Jesuits at the colleges of Bologna, Modena, Brescia, Forli, Ferrara, Padua, Parma, Piacenza, and Verona, and their offices. Still older is *News of the Colleges of the Province of Lombardy, March 1573*,[24] that has a full report on the state of the provinces of Milan and Venice, which from 1558 to 1578 were parts of the Lombardy (or Cisalpine) province. It records that there were then twelve colleges, two professed houses, and two novice houses. Next, side by side, are reports on the first foundations of the colleges, on their endowments (donations of sufficient income from a benefactor, who assumed the title of founder, and was deemed especially deserving of recognition by the Society), later gifts and other events, as well as specific items about income and expenses, and the condition of the building and school. The professors and other religious are listed, along with their academic assignments (offices), e.g., rector. At times the college received money earmarked for teaching certain disciplines, and that also was recorded.

Of course, very few documents from the first decades of the Society's existence are as clear and complete as these. Many notes, lists, and tables up to the end of the 1500s are fragmentary or incomplete and difficult to disentangle. ARSI archivists have patiently and diligently published them all with delicate and wise restoration and conservation work in the volumes *Informationes antiquae* (catalogs and notices of the years 1554-1602), *Catalogi antiquissimi collegiorum Italiae* (1546-77, some to 1600), *Status et numerus 1574* (the whole world, by province),[25] and some others.

More heterogeneous and less directly useful are the sources for mathematics teaching in the individual colleges. A catalog of notices of institution of chairs, course content, frequency of lectures, or relations with the ambient cultural scene, necessarily involves search of local archival sources, and, in particular, identification and use of data from Jesuit universities like Genoa, Milan, and Parma that the state seized at the Suppression of the Society. ARSI has histories of the colleges written by the Jesuits themselves. For the provinces that interest us we have the *Storia del Collegio di Genova da' suoi principi nel 1553 fino al 1772 scritta dal P. Nicolò Gentile, e dal 1689 continuata da vari,* and the *Informatione dello stato del collegio di S. Lucia di Bologna data dall'anno 1580 al presente del 1673.*[26] But data is scarce about teaching because the histories relate, in succinct analytic form, facts about the college as a whole. News of gifts, ceremonies, debts, building condition, and internal and external conflict predominates.[27]

Papers and letters of the Jesuit teachers and scientists are of greater interest. They comprise the main source for the instructional content and history of the college chairs. In particular, it seems only from these letters can we learn adequately about the actual interrelationship between the teaching and personal study and research of the Society's better scientists, a topic the importance of which needs no emphasis. Its many facets are little explored, for example, the criteria that determined the choice of an instructor or the future of a student. It is a question not only of learning how often the same person was both scientist and teacher, but also of noting how many scholars, known by their publications, also taught or held other offices. One has to estimate the link between teaching and new scientific productivity, what it is and when it occurred, and do this, most of all, starting from the experience of the teaching scientist, also to estimate how much the need for advanced research and the duty of teaching in the Jesuit schools were effectively concurrent, or at least compatible. This way only can we hope to shed light *from the inside* on how the roles that the Society undertook in the field of science were related, how it related to civil and religious society, and the place it had, objectively, in the development of society and culture, both European and non-European.

Among the more noted and important unedited collections are the correspondence of Christopher Clavius and Athanasius Kircher preserved in the archives of the Pontifical Gregorian University. E. C. Phillips published a catalog of Clavius' letters: "The Correspondence of Fr. Chr. Clavius Preserved in the Archives of the Pont. Gregorian University."[28]

Very useful for identifying instructional matter are the lecture notes and other didactic material made or kept by students and instructors; these may be profitably used for comparisons with printed works and current manuals. An example of the latter is *Brevis introductio in totam mathematicam per Patrem Iacobum Bonvicinum Neapolitanum,* preserved in the manuscript collection of the Bibliotheca Universitaria of Genoa.[29] Giacomo Bonvicino, who taught mathematics at the college of Genoa from 1652 to 1656, and died of the plague in 1657, edited *Brevis introductio* in 1654, but did not circulate it, nor is he identified with this or any other work in the Order's bibliographical index. *Brevis introductio* has 160 14.5 x 21 cm. pages, and is divided into four parts. The first has 36 geometry problems and two short notes ("On the angle of incidence equal to an angle," and "What is a direction line?"). The second part treats trigonometry ("A brief treatise of trigonometry"). The third has astronomy, with mention of general terrestrial geography ("Brief explanation of the content of the Sphere"). The fourth part looks at the problem of statics ("Mechanics"). Pedagogical expository arrangement was explicit: "To follow natural order which always starts from easier things, we must do some exercises before we try deep mathematics and geometry. We will therefore give without explanation many problems that will be developed later in the Euclid lectures."[30] This practical and didactic purpose is precisely what constitutes three centuries later the central point of interest here and in similar texts.

We began by indicating that up to now such important topics as the teaching of scientific disciplines in the larger modern European school organization had been neglected. Now there are good possibilities for ending that neglect. Systematic study of material such as we have found will surely illuminate the circumstances and structures that drove the actual historical development of modern science.

NOTES

1. "After the Society decided to admit also young men who had yet to be trained in letters, and to open colleges with their own schools, it had to choose whether to follow the *modus italicus* or the *modus parisiensis* in its schools" (L. Lukacs, *Monumenta Paedagogica, Nova editio ex integro rejecta, 1540-1556*, Roma, 1965, p. 616).

2. See M. Barbera, *S.I., La Ratio studiorum e la parte IV delle Costituzioni della Compagnia di Gesù*, Padua, 1942: "The *modus parisiensis* had two principal characteristics. The first was the distinction of class and course levels, so that the students attend to one thing at a time, and progress in an orderly way. There were, in particular, five classes in the humanities course. The second characteristic was that the professors gave special supervision to the students with many and rigorous exercises. In Italy, on the other hand, solemnity and pomp prevailed in instruction given from the lofty heights of the chair to students and auditors of diverse competence, without the professor being obligated to the students or to the advantage of the youth" (p. xx).

3. P. O. Kristeller, *La tradizione classica nel pensiero del Rinascimento*, Firenze, 1965, pp. 42-43.

4. *Constitutiones Societatis Iesu cum earum declarationibus*, Romae, MDLXXXIII, Parte IV, cap. XII, par. 3.

5. Ibid., Parte IV, cap. XIV, par. 3.

6. C. Clavius, *Modus quo disciplinae mathematicae in scholis Societatis possent promoveri*, in *Monumenta Paedagogica Societatis Iesu*, quae primam Rationem studiorum anno 1586 editam praecessere, Madrid, 1901, pp. 472 ff.

7. Ibid.

8. "All the philosophers, in the second year of philosophy, will hear the mathematics lectures in the school for three quarters of an hour. Let those apt and inclined to such studies be trained after the course with private lectures" (*Ratio atque institutio studiorum, 1599*, Cap. I, Regole del Provinciale, 20, in Barbera, *op. cit.*, p. 126).

9. See M. Scaduto, "Il matematico Francesco Maurolico e i gesuiti," *AHSI* 18 (1949), pp. 126-41.

10. The *Ratio studiorum* took advantage of a wealth of practical experience, as well as theoretic and programmatic discussion held over more than a half-century of uninterrupted and growing instructional activity everywhere, including Reformation lands and

non-European locales (East and West Indies, China, etc.). As already noted, the Jesuits first undertook instruction of extern students at the college of Goa, in India, that Diego de Borba had already established there right after the arrival of St. Francis Xavier, who in 1542 asked and got from St. Ignatius some instructors to teach humanities and Christian doctrine to Indian and Portuguese youths. Jesuit missionaries taught there from 1543 to 1549 when they had complete direction of it. (Barbera, *op. cit.,* p. 27, note 1.) No discussion of the Society of Jesus can prescind from the universal scope of its presence and from the demands that its vast missionary activity in its contact with heretics and non-Christian peoples put on the whole organization in matters of education and cultural policy. In the circumstances, mathematics and science in general were taken among the most efficacious means to establish contact with a hostile, or at least foreign, environment. St. Ignatius himself used to say that "Our Society in its desire to help souls will seize the spoils of Egypt to turn them to the honor and glory of God, because in our day (the humanities) are quite necessary to make progress with souls, *especially in northern regions* (italics ours)" *(Momumenta Ignatiana,* First Series, *Sancti Ignatii de Loyola epistolae et instructiones*, I-XII, Madrid, 1903-11, VIII, letter 618 of 30 March 1555). Ignatius here refers to the study of classical humanities, Cicero and Demosthenes, but his argument is also valid for the sciences. Indeed, in India and China, only the latter will do. To be sure, this necessarily created among many Jesuit scholars a turn toward the external and a mindset somewhat heterodox and unfamiliar in the milieu of the Counter-Reformation.

The definitive version of the rule of studies in the Society's colleges was completed in 1598, but it was sent to the press only in 1599: *Ratio atque institutio studiorum Societatis Iesu,* Napoli, in collegio eiusdem Societatis. Ex typographia Tarquinii Longii, MDXCVIII, then, Napoli, apud Tarquinium Longium, MDIC. It was preceded, as is known, by two other drafts, the first published in 1586 *(Ratio atque institutio studiorum per sex Patrem ad id iussu R P. Generalis deputatos conscripta,* Romae, in Collegio Societatis Iesu, MDLXXXVI), the second in 1591 *(Ratio atque Institutio Studiorum,* Romae, in Collegio Societatis Iesu, MDXCI). The 1599 *Ratio,* slightly amended by the Seventh General Congregation (1615) was reprinted in 1616, and was ever afterwards entered in the editions of *Institutum Societatis Iesu.* In addition to the text in the *Institutum,* there is the edition edited by G. M. Pachtler: *Ratio studiorum et institutiones scholasticae Societatis Iesu per Germaniam olim vigentes,* I-IV, Berlin, 1887-94 *(–Monumenta Germaniae Paedagogica);* this also has the first *Ratio.* By contrast, the 1591 *Ratio* was not reprinted, and original copies are almost nonexistent: "The original edition must have had very few copies, because extant ones are exceedingly rare. One is in the Library of London (not in the British Museum), another in the Cambridge University Library, a third in the Jesuit scholasticate at Louvain" (Barbera, *op. cit.,* p. 45.) Barbera and Allan P. Farrell (*The Jesuit Code of Liberal Education. Development and Scope of the Ratio Studiorum,* Milwaukee, 1938, from which this data comes) overlook the copy existing in the ARSI, which I was able to consult, thanks to the courtesy of Fr. Edmund Lamalle, director of the archives. It was Superior General Claude Acquaviva's copy, with many annotations in his hand. On some blank pages in the back of the volume, there was copied a little manuscript treatise *De delectu opinionum,* a topic debated at the time by the Commission for the *Ratio studiorum* ("When they were appointed to redo the *Ratio studiorum,* and, after precise discussion and debate for many days, they sent to the Congregation their judgment about the speculative part and the selection of [theological] opinions, the Congregation approved their decisions" [*Institutum Societatis Iesu,* Firenze, 1893, IL p. 272]); this was marked out in the *Regulae pro delectu opinionum* approved by the Fifth General Congregation meeting between 3 November 1593 and 18 January 1594. The *acta* of the General Congregations are published in *Institutum, op. cit.*

The official text that preceded the *Ratio* was developed from the *Constitutions* composed by St. Ignatius; their Fourth Part treated the ordinance on studies: chapters 11-17 on the universities date to the years 1553-54 (See *Mon. Paed.* nova editio, *op. cit.,* p. 271). The *Constitutions* were approved by the First General Congregation in 1558.

The chapter *De mathematicis* of the 1586 *Ratio* begins appropriately with citation of Declaration C attached to the passage cited of the *Contstitutions* (see n. 4): "Logic, physics, metaphysics, moral science, and mathematics too will be taught to the extent they help to the goal proposed to us." The Fourth General

Congregation (February-April 1581) ordered preparation of an edition of the *Constitutions* that was issued in 1583; it was used for the passages given here. By decree of the General Congregation it became the official text of the Society's fundamental law.

We must note here, however briefly, some documents written before and after the *Constitutions* that have particular importance for the history of mathematics instruction. First, the *Constitutiones Collegii Messanensis (1548)* and the *De studii generalis dispositione et ordine (1552)*, both by Father Jerome Nadal. They have been published in the oft cited first (and up to now the only published) volume of the new series *Monumenta Paedagogica* that records documents up to 1556. But for the period between the drafting of the Ignatian *Constitutions* and the first *Ratio*, there are important manuscripts attributed both to Christopher Clavius, from which we took the passage printed in the text, and Geralamo Torres; all are published in the single volume of the old *Mon. Paed;* these too have already been cited. Those of Clavius are two brief handwritten texts, the first is entitled *Modus quo disciplinae mathematicae etc.*, (see note 6 above), while the editors of *Mon. Paed.* gave the title *De re mathematica instructio* to the second, which is untitled in the manuscript. Also, the very brief Torres manuscripts (each a page) are in Spanish, but have Latin titles: *De studiis mathematicis,* and *De rebus mathematicis.*

See G. Cosentino, "Mathematics in the Jesuit *Ratio studiorum*," in this volume, pp. 47-79, for pedagogical documents relative to the teaching of mathematics in Jesuit schools.

11. For northern Italy there is just A. Monti, *La Compagnia di Gesù nel territorio della Provincia Torinese,* 5 vols., Chien, 1914-20. Only the first volume treats the period before 1773 (the old Society). Some other histories of the Society's Italian provinces are E. Aguileia, *Provinciae Siculae Societatis Iesu ortus et res gestae,* 2 vols., Palermo, 1737-40 (comprising the period from 1546 to 1672); F. Schinosi, *Istoria della Compagnia di Gesù appartenente al Regno di Napoli,* 2 vols., Napoli, 1706-11 (from 1538 to 1600), continued by S. Santagata, 2 vols., Napoli, 1756-57 (from 1600 to 1650); G. Barella, *La Compagnia di Gesù nelle Puglie,* 1574-1767, 1635-1940, Lecce, 1941; A. Arami, *Storia della Compagnia di Gesù in Sardegna,* Genova, 1939 (from 1552 to 1938). For the Society of Jesus in Italy, see P. Tacchi Venturi, *Storia della Compagnia di Gesù*

in Italia, narrata col sussidio di fonti inedite, 2 vols. in 4 sections, Rome, 1910 (vol. primo, 1ª ed.), 1922-52 (vol. secundo, 1º & 2ᵈᵒ t., respectively). The first volume treats religious life in Italy during the first era of the Society, the second has the life of Ignatius Loyola, the foundation of the Society, and its history up to his death (1491-56). This now classic work was continued by M. Scaduto, *L'epoca di Giacomo Laínez, il Governo (1556-65),* Rome, 1964. All the works cited present the major events of the Society and its houses and colleges from a general point of view. Only in passing do they have items about teaching. Their value for the history of mathematics teaching is solely in providing a frame of reference for the stages of such instruction as known from other sources.

12. F. De Dainville, S.J., "L'enseignement des mathématiques dans les Collèges Jésuites de France du XVIᵉ au XVIIIᵉ siècle," *Revue d'histoire des sciences et de leurs application 7,* nn. 1-2 (January-June 1954), pp. 6-21, 102-23, and "L'Enseignement scientifique dans les Collèges des Jésuites," in *Enseignement et diffusion des sciences in France au XVIIIᵉ siècle,* Paris, 1964, pp. 27-65.

13. Rome, 1954.

14. *AHSI* 17 (1948), pp. 102-59.

15. Firenze, 1969.

16. "The primary purpose of both archives (i.e., of the old Society up to 1773 and of the 'restored' Society from 1814) was and is to serve the Superior General and his assistants in the government of the Order. A second purpose is to help the portrayal of events or history. And so for good reason, use of the documents is ordinarily restricted to Very Reverend Father General, unless about a hundred years have elapsed" (G. Teschitel, "Archivum Romanum Societatis Iesu *[ARSI],*" *Archivum* 4 [1954], p. 145). In this article, the author, who was director of the Society's general archives, gives a brief prospectus or summary of the archives, a clear classification of the material of great use for a first orientation. See also the same author's "L'organizzazione dell'archivo generale della Compagnia di Gesù," *Rassegna degli Archivi di Stato* 22 (1962), pp. 189-96. For the origin of the archives, see G. Schurhammer, "Die Anfänge des Römischen Archivs der Gesellschaft Jesu (1538-1548)," AHSI 12 (1943), pp. 88-118.

17. "Because of the differences in their juridical status, the Roman Archives and the Fondo Gesuitico were not combined, but set side

by side, under the same archivist, and keep their different classifications." E. Lamalle, "L'inventaire des plans des Archives romaines de la Compagnie," in J. Vallery-Radot, *La recueil de plans d'edifices de la Compagnie de Jésus conservé à la Bibliothèque Nationale de Paris,* Roma, 1960, p. 396.

18. "In the booklet *Regularum PP. Mercuriani et Aquavivae* there is preserved the *Formula scribendi...* that was expanded by P. Acquaviva" (A. Coemans, *Breves notitiae de Instituto, historia, bibliographia Societatis,* 2nd ed. revised and expanded, Brussells, 1937, p. 42). Mercurian's *Formula* is in ARSI Inst. 40, ff. 77-78 (Formula conficiendorum catalogorum missa ad provincias in principio anni 1579); here can also be found Acquaviva's corrections and additions (ff. 114-114v: Formula catalogorum conficiendorurn, recognita calendris novembris 1589, and ibid. f 139: De emendatione seu additione ad formulam catalogorum, ut catalogi singulis suis nominibus appellentur, Calendris octobris 1590.) The definitive *Formula scribendi* has been published in *Institutum Societatis Iesu, op. cit.,* III, pp. 36ff.

19. From Ven 71 to Ven 91a (province of Venice), and from Med 1 to Med 19 (province of Milan). The annual catalogs were usually compiled at the start of the scholastic year (October-November), and always had the inscription *exeunte anno...,* with the date of the year in progress, or perhaps *ineunte anno...,* with the date of the following year. The catalogs always have a list of Jesuit students who were attending the higher courses of theology, and also of those who were hearing philosophy.

20. "First, for each one record his name and family name, his country, age, health, years in the Society, studies and ministries undertaken, academic degrees, if any, whether professed or coadjutor, etc., and when. In the second catalog list the man's talents and qualities, that is, his intellectual ability, judgment, prudence, experience, progress in letters, ordinary demeanor, and what talents he has for the Society's ministries" (*Formula scribendi,* nn. 32-33, in *Institutum, op. cit.,* III, p. 45).

21. "The number of Ours in each house should be recorded, and also how many of them are priests, professors, scholastics, and in what faculties; how many are temporal coadjutors, what is [the house's] income, what ordinary alms it gets, how much money is borrowed..." (*De catalogis, qui tertio quoque anno a singulis*

provinciis in urbem mitti debent. R. P. N. Claudii Aquavivae Praepositi Generalis, iussu recognita, et anno 1580 in Provincias missa. In *Institutum, op. cit.* III, p. 309).

22. The triennial catalogs of the Venetian and Milanese provinces came from Ven 37 to Ven 62, and Med 47 to Med 69, respectively.

23. Ven 37a.

24. Ven 36a.

25. Hist. Soc. 175; Rom. 78b; Hist. Soc. 41.

26. Med 80 and Ven 112.

27. Analogous considerations hold for the *Annuae Litterae,* with edifying content for the most part. These were published, starting from those of 1581 up to the ones of 1653-54: *Annuae Litterae Societatis Iesu anni...ad Patres et Fratres eiusdem Societatis,* 36 vols. The first was published in Rome, the last at Prague in 1658.

28. In AHSI 8 (1939), pp. 193-222. The list is not error free. For Kircher's correspondence, see G. Gabrieli, "Carteggi Kircheriani," in *Regia Academia d'Italia, Rendiconti di scienze morali e storiche,* 7th series, 2 (1949), pp. 10-17. Among the most interesting and topically related are a group of letters of Jesuit mathematics teachers found in the Biblioteca Nazionale di Firenze among the Galilean manuscripts. There are letters of Vincenzo Viviani and a good number of letters of Ferroni, and some others of Riccioli, Lana Terzi, Ceva, Saccheri, Boscovich, and Riccati. Saccheri's two letters to Viviani were edited by A. Favaro, *Due lettere inedite di G. Saccheri a V. Viviani,* Paris, 1903.

29. Mss. F. VI 6.

30. Ibid. p. 5.